WALTZING WITH GOD IN THE GARDENS OF OUR HEARTS

Tamara M. Gunn

Blessings!
Tamara Gunn
Num 6:24-26

Purpose Publishing
1503 Main Street #168 ♁ Grandview, Missouri
www.purposepublishing.com

Copyright © 2017 Tammy Gunn

ISBN: 978-0-9997999-8-7

Editing by Felicia Murrell
Book Cover artwork by Michael Schneider

All scripture contained in this book are referenced from the New King James Version, The Message, New Living Translation, Amplified and New International Versions of the Bible.

Printed in the United States of America.

CONTENTS

DEDICATION

This book belongs to the Prince of Peace who in my childhood, stepped into my broken world and gave me peace in those days of pain and sorrow. Like the stars touching heaven, I was allowed to grasp a small glimpse of that special place.

In certain places of my heart, time stood still causing decay in my life. However, one day, my Prince of Peace rode in on His white stallion and started the process of removing all the rotting decay that surrounded my life. He replaced it with a freshness only He could bring.

My Prince of Peace held my hands gently and step by step He walked me through the barriers of time to heal those painful places that had broken my heart. Then He filled those places up with His love and my soul was set free to run after Him completely.

Now, I can run into His arms with no shame, singing a new song of freedom that He has given me. As we embrace, my heart floods with joy for the Lover of my soul. My Prince of Peace has me in His loving arms again.

He whispers in my ear, "Dance with Me, My love." As we waltz, I know in my heart our dance will go on throughout eternity in the wonderful garden He has created for me.

INTRODUCTION

Our hearts are like many gardens. We can let them grow to be places of refuge where there is only peace, joy, and love or we can let them be filled with bitterness, hatred, and unforgiveness. What we do with the things in our past that have broken and hurt us is always our choice.

By the time I realized my heart's garden was a total mess, I was a grown woman, married with four children. I had been walking with the Lord for many years but I had no idea I was really broken inside. I knew I had lived with fear, doubt, and unbelief all the time but I never knew why.

All I knew was that my personal choice was to build up walls of protection to feel safe. But the truth is I never did. I had put everyone who ever hurt me behind a wall with a lock and key. I never let myself or anyone else enter those places because it was very painful.

I walked around as a Christian woman serving the Lord. With all my heart, that's who I thought I was, but that was only a very small portion of my life. I was consumed by self-hatred to the extent that I could not even look in the mirror. I was very angry inside.

In the twinkling of an eye, the Prince of Peace stepped into my heart's garden and began a work that has changed me forever. He took a woman trapped in the emotional bondage of a little girl who had been abused, abandoned, rejected, and broken. A little girl who lost her innocence. A little girl who grew up all broken inside stuck in a grown-up body but stunted by the brokenness of childhood.

Like flower seeds, He stepped into my heart's garden and began to replant it with His love. He so graciously entered my world touching every area of anger, fear, and rejection. As I gave Him full access to my garden He uprooted all the bitterness and anger that was there. He took all the fear, doubt and unbelief out leaving joy, peace and love. As I gave Him full access to my life, one step at a time He healed them all. He has replaced all those bitter seeds of hate with love. Rather than hate those who hurt me in the past, I felt compassion for them.

The Prince of Peace longs to do the same in your heart. Ask yourself what is growing in your heart's garden. Can you examine your heart without fear or do you run and hide from your hurt and pain thinking no one would ever know? That is what I did but I was so wrong because the Prince of Peace knew.

If I had not allowed heaven's rain to fall on me, I would never have known there was such peace to be had. I would have remained that little girl in emotional bondage, trapped forever. My heart was a place of no rest or peace. I had no idea what real peace even was. As a matter of fact, I was even afraid of having peace because I feared it and did not know what to expect.

It took time but when I finally unlocked the gates and allowed my Prince of peace to enter in life returned to my garden and me. It was an awesome thing to behold as I watched the overflowing love of God change me. It has been an amazing journey.

I can close my eyes now and whisper His wonderful name and I am there in the midst of that beautiful place He has created for me, waiting for Him to come. I never wait long because at the whisper of His name Jesus He is right beside me. I stand in the midst of my garden now and look around to see nothing but beauty. My arms outstretched to the side looking up to the heavens as the sun pours down upon me. His love and joy flood my soul as the rain of heaven falls in a midst around me. I know now that all His promises are true. There are no more broken places left unturned. He has conquered them all. He has restored all the Enemy has stolen.

When I look in the mirror today I no longer see a little girl all broken inside or one who always thought she was so ugly that no one would ever love her. Now I see a beautiful woman who is complete and knows she is loved by the Prince of

Peace, Jesus. I finally know that He had rode in on His white stallion and conquered those broken places in my heart. The Prince of Peace, Jesus, also desires to heal your brokenness. He wants to help you put the pieces back together and heal your heart.

In writing this book, it is my hope that you will be encouraged to remove the walls you have set up to protect you from being hurt again and give access to the Prince of Peace, Jesus, to heal you.

As you read each page, may you be touched by His love, and healing power. He will create a garden full of love, peace and joy. A garden were we can meet with Him daily seeking His will for our lives. A place were the cares of this world are left laying at His feet. He will create a place in your heart where you are forever free. A place where we are in the boat of life and He says, "Let's go to the other side," and "Peace be still." We trust Him to take us there. We can then run into His arms and as He embraces us and whispers in our ear "Dance with me my love" we waltz off into the setting sun knowing He has us in His loving embrace.

CHAPTER 1

BROKEN BUT FIXABLE

Life's journey is on a road paved with ups and downs! In spite of that, I love life in the Lord because He is constantly pushing me to change. God wants us to become more than we are in the broken places that are frozen in our minds. And so, I must be obedient to Him to become the woman He has called me to be. When He formed me in my mother's womb, He wrote down my days in the book of life (Psalms 139). He wants us to fulfill the destiny He has planned for us.

Sometimes, in our lives, we can get side-tracked along the way; however, He is always faithful to bring us back to the places He has called us to be.

At times, we have to find healing on those broken roads and although it can be a difficult process, I promise you, it's possible. As you learn how to surrender to His will, you will be healed as I was. Your journey can become an adventure.

In my life, I have walked several roads that I have had to surrender to God. Although I may not have accomplished many things in the world's eyes, I am very rich with the love of the Lord inside me; at times, I cannot contain myself. I feel as if I will burst with joy for all the things He has brought me through.

Each road we walk in our lives is a journey through a new season. Sometimes, those seasons go by quickly while at other times, the transition is very long and painful. It is the difficult seasons that show we made it through only by God's grace and mercy.

The long painful seasons usually involve testing that draws us closer to God and teaches us to trust Him. John 15: 13 says that when we abide in Him and His words abide in us, we can ask what we will, and He will do it for us. What a promise! Most often, these times test us to see if we are willing to surrender our wills to His. He draws us closer so we will know how to trust and obey when life gets really hard.

I have to admit that I have fallen many times on these journeys. I thought the road was too difficult and chose to give up. Of course, eventually, I would have to do it all over again. Every time I have fallen, the Lord never scolded me. No, He only poured more love on me and always encouraged me so I could make it through the next time. He continued to pick me up and carry me on the hardest roads I have faced.

Now, I have learned how to rest and abide in Him each and every day. Sometimes, I wonder why He chose me or why He even loves me. But He has stuck with me even when I just wanted to sit down and quit. Those scars froze me into believing I was not worthy. Many times we have weeds growing in our hearts that we have chosen to hold on to. We have to allow Jesus in to those places so we can be healed.

Man will never see what God has placed in my heart to do for Him but that no longer matters. All that matters is what the Lord has called me to do. Many need to know how much God loves them. He wants to heal them from all the broken things in their past as He has done me. He wants to let them know that although they may be broken, they are fixable, whether they need financial, physical, emotional or spiritual healing, He can do it.

The Enemy has no right to speak to the children of God

Sometimes, I would take my eyes off God and the Enemy would step into my thoughts reminding me of my past and all my failures. He has always done that, unlike God, who says I am a child of the King, and I am a daughter of the Most High God. I was purchased with a great price and the Enemy has no right to speak to me.

The problem is it took me a long time to learn that if you open a door for the Enemy, he will bombard you with self-defeating thoughts that will run wild in your minds. He wants to kill, steal, and totally destroy us. Therefore, we must know who we are in Christ and the Enemy has no right to us.

I am at the point in my life where I refuse to let the Enemy rob me of my peace and joy. I still have journeys to walk but now I walk them with great peace. On your way to healing, you must take every thought that is not from God captive. If you want to be healed, bring your negative thoughts to the Lord. Take the words of your mouth and examine what you are saying. Proverbs 18:21 says we have the power of death and life in our tongue, and we eat the words of it, either for death or life. Speak life and know that God loves you so very much. He wants you to be well!

God's Word is life to us. As we read and apply it to whatever road we might be on, we will always have peace and strength for the journey. We also must have faith for this journey. Hebrews 12: 1 says that without faith it is impossible to please God. Faith moves mountains. Faith makes the impossible become possible. If we have faith as small as a mustard seed, we can say to this mountain, "Be removed!" and it has to go. With God nothing is impossible! We must believe more than we see until Jesus comes back for us.

We also need hope to keep going on. Without hope, our hearts become weary and tired. Hope believes that things will get better as we walk through life's journeys. Finally, the most important thing is love. If we do not love, then we do not know God. Loving unconditionally can be a challenge, especially when we have been wronged.

1 Corinthians 13:4-8 has been one of my life scriptures since I was saved as a young girl. I believe God put that scripture before me when I was young because He knew it would be a hard road I would have to walk. This scripture helped me realize that love and forgiveness are the greatest gifts we can give to others who have hurt us and also to ourselves.

We are filled with great peace when we allow the Lord to fill us with His love. When we forgive someone who has wronged or betrayed us, an awesome transformation takes place in our hearts. We can finally see how much Jesus did for us on the cross when He died. He forgave us so it is only right to forgive and love others as much as He has loved us.

God gives us the strength to forgive and walk on through the hard days. Find yourself in your prayer closet seeking the Lord with all your heart, soul, and mind. When you are there with Him, ask Him if there is anyone you need to forgive. Ask Him if there are frozen memories of your past. Ask Him, and He will very lovingly take you by the hand and show you the way. Most of us already know what needs to be healed in us. The problem is we feel we are alone and there is no one to reach out to for help. But you must remember that you are never alone.

Several years ago, as I spoke and shared my testimony, I began to wonder if it had touched anyone's life. No one came forward for prayer so I ended the service and prayed for everyone to have a safe trip home. I was hugging each one as I normally did when an older lady who was probably in her late seventies came and hugged me. She whispered in my ear, "I was molested when I was a child too." She then said, "I have never told anyone this before till you." I hugged her again and prayed healing would come. God did that for her. You never know whose life you will touch.

Chapter 2

THE JOURNEY

My journey began on June 25, 1959. The day I was born, my momma was alone because my dad had already left her for another woman. He had cheated on her with her best friend. My mom's heart was broken. He left her with three children under the age of five to raise on her own. If my grandparents were not there for us, I am sure we probably would have ended up in a home somewhere. My dad went on with his life and really did not seem to care if the family God gave him was okay or not.

My mom had to work so much that my grandparents had to take care of us. I became my grandpa's girl. He took me everywhere with him. He was a funeral plot salesman and did a lot of traveling to different areas. Many times, I rode along. My grandparents only attended church occasionally. My mom took us to church when she could but there was really no teaching of God in our home. Because my mom was so hurt over my dad leaving her, she started looking for someone to fill that spot in her heart.

She dated men who always abused her and also treated us badly. One of my first memories is of a man holding me over a toilet when I was about three and telling me he was going to flush me. I have a lot of bad memories about my life from birth to age nine. However, I also have some fun memories of my mom and my brothers. Although my mom lived her life with all the pain and hurt she suffered from my dad, she did the best she could for us.

The first time I remember hearing about Jesus was when I was about four years old. At that time, I asked Him to come into my heart. I think I was a seer in the spirit from that point on. I would see myself in a garden sitting on a swing just having a great talk with my Jesus. That place where I would go in my heart became my place of escape on a daily basis. When my days were filled with too many challenges for me to handle as a little girl, I would run there and into His arms. It was a beautiful garden filled with roses and flowers of every kind and my Jesus was there.

I had no idea until years later that the Lord had given me a glimpse of what my heart's garden looked like before it became corrupted with so much pain. At that time, the garden was just filled with His presence, and He tended to it. When I was a little girl, I always had the same dream most girls have.

That dream was to be a beautiful bride all dressed in white with long, flowing hair full of pretty flowers. I always saw myself waltzing with a man

(Jesus) dressed in a long white robe with a beautiful crown on His head. I knew this was my Prince who would love me forever. He would take my hand in His and we would dance around the room. My heart would feel such great joy in those moments. In that place of joy, the world would seem so far away and time just stood still. When I looked into His eyes, I knew in my heart He was someone I could trust. I knew those eyes had touched my very soul.

Somehow, I just knew I could trust that man in my dream world. There was something about His eyes that captured my heart. I felt if I could just keep my eyes fixed on Him, I could make it. As He took my hand in His, we waltzed through all the pain I was feeling at the time. For a few minutes, I was able to forget everything I had gone through. Dancing off into the sunset, peace, and joy would come again and flood my soul. I knew at that point I could make it through another day. I knew I could always come back to the place where my Prince was always waiting for me.

It took me years to realize that the Lord had given me this time with Him so that I would not hold bitterness in my heart, and I would know again that I could trust Him. He would step in and heal all the broken and hurting places in my heart. When He stepped back into my heart years later, I finally realized He really had never left. I had just stopped going to that place to talk with Him. I had locked Him behind a wall out of fear.

When He stepped back into my life once again, I allowed Him to take my hands. As we waltzed together, and I looked into those eyes, once again trust was restored. I knew I had to take a chance and allow Him to help me. As I began this journey with Him in my forties that took several years to complete, I had to learn how to trust Him again. I became a worshiper. In His presence, I found peace and great joy. He became my strength and my hope.

In my childhood, I constantly feared my mom was never coming back because she did not love or want me. From birth, I was always being left with my grandparents. I know now she had no choice but back then, I believed it was my fault. Always feeling unloved and unwanted brought feelings of fear and rejection into my life.

The pain of my mom rejecting me made me fear her, and I believe those feelings started in her womb. Throughout my childhood, I felt she loved my brothers more than me, and I always tried to do everything to please her. However, the more I tried, the more it seemed like she pushed me away. It seemed like my mom just did not know how to love me. I thought I was always a reminder of what my dad had done to her and that's why she often left me with my grandparents.

I was a constant reminder of my dad because I looked like him and had a lot of his personality traits. I was that thorn in her side as a reminder that he had cheated on her with her best friend while she was pregnant with me. It was a very painful scar she carried with her all her life. She never could forgive him for that pain he caused her. It was so severe, it caused her to be angry at

26

me most of the time. Everything I did was wrong in her eyes.

That pain in her heart also caused her to look for love in all the wrong places. She found my stepfather in one of those places. He not only physically and verbally abused my mom but he also abused my brothers and me.

By the time I was two, my dad had moved on with his life. He remarried a woman he had met and was living for himself. This was not the woman he had cheated on my mom with. He would collect my brothers for a visit but I was never allowed to go. I believe she kept me from my dad because he had rejected her so much, and it was her way of protecting me. On the other hand, at times, I felt it was vengeance.

I do not think my dad wanted me anyway. Before I was born, he said he never wanted any more children and that is why he left my mom. I had no relationship with him until I was eighteen and that was only because I pushed it on him. Every time he told me the stories of how and why he left my mom, it would break my heart more for her. To me, he was only making excuses for the life he chose to have without us.

Each time he said he did not want any more children and he told my mom that, I heard in my heart it was me he never wanted. I never told him how much hearing that hurt me. Sometimes, people who are supposed to love and treasure you can be so hurtful and heartbreaking.

When my mom married my stepfather, I was probably five years old. We lived around the corner from my grandparents. Each day, my brothers and I were dropped off for my grandma to take care of us. My stepfather would usually pick us up after work. Sometimes, he would just pick me up. Home for me was what everyone in the family thought was supposed to be a happy little home full of kids. Instead, it was a house of horror!

I was so afraid of my stepfather I knew not to cross him. If I did, off came that belt, and I was beaten again. From the first time he touched me inappropriately, and I said, "No!" I was beaten with that belt. He threatened to kill my mom, brothers, and my grandparents if I told anyone. He told me he would take my grandpa's guns and shoot us all. I was truly at his mercy because I believed he would do what he said. Everything I did seemed to be a reason for him to beat me. It was a reminder of what he would do if I ever told what he was doing to me daily.

I would run down to the basement and hide in the corner after he finished doing all he wanted to me and beating me with that belt for struggling and fighting with him. Many times, my legs would be bleeding from the beating. Fear would consume me, and I would shake all over. My lips would quiver as I cried and cried for it just to end. I would cry so hard but no one ever came and rescued me from that horrible place. As I sat there crying, I would hear my Prince calling me to come and sit awhile with Him. So I would go to my place of escape and run into His arms of love where He was always waiting for me. My dream world was truly my only place of refuge.

Many days, it was not only my stepfather molesting me but also my stepbrothers. If I told on them, I feared I'd be accused of lying. I was threatened by them also to not tell anyone. I did not want to be beaten by that belt again so I just took their abuse. I began to believe that I was never going to escape the torture. I endured days of not only being sexually abused but also verbally abused. I was told I was fat, ugly, stupid, and unwanted. And you know what? I believed it. My family members who were supposed to love and protect me were the very ones who insulted me and crushed my self-esteem.

Finally, I went to school at six years old and felt like an outcast. I carried an abundance of shame and always felt very different from all the rest of the kids. I felt I had no friends, unloved, and unwanted. I was extremely backward and shy. I was afraid of everyone. I had a hard time learning to read and every other subject was extremely hard for me.

So many days, my mom seemed to destroy the hopes and dreams of the little girl in me who just wanted her daddy to come and rescue her. Even though I really did not know him, I dreamed he would be my hero. I always believed my daddy loved me even though I was told constantly he did not. My mom consistently filled my head with hateful words about my dad. In my eyes, he looked like a monster but deep inside, I still wanted to know him. It would take me several years before I would ever do so. Even then, it was at a distance because of my stepmom. My days were filled with nothing but pain and hurt.

I built towering walls in my heart hoping they would protect me against those who hurt me. I locked up the painful memories and lost the little girl inside me, somewhere. I built wall upon wall, not only to protect myself but also to hide the shame I felt. In those days the only one who knew me was my Prince in that dream world where I escaped. I always hoped I could just stay there with Him so I would never have to go back to that pain again. I never wanted them to know the real me. I feared they would hate me because I thought everything that was happening to me was my fault. Even at my young age, I knew I could never tell anyone my plight. They would never understand. In those days, children were to be seen and never heard. I had no voice! Children were never to say anything against adults. If I had spoken up at that time, no one would have believed me.

Even after I told my grandpa I felt such shame. I took all those memories and buried them so deep inside my heart's dungeon that no one would be able to find them for years to come. Jesus always knew they were there, but He was so good to me that He took His time healing all those wounds.

I knew the only place I could ever feel safe was in my secret garden with my Prince of Peace. I could run into that place any time I needed to back then. I would just close my eyes and see myself in the midst of that beautiful garden. There were wild flowers of blue, pink, yellow and purple growing everywhere along with beautiful roses. The sky was so blue, and the sun shone down so brightly.

I would never see myself as dirty and broken there with my Prince. I was always in a pretty, soft pink dress with my hair full of flowers and the gentle breeze blowing gently on my face. I would stand in that secret place and breathe in all of its beauty. I wanted to keep that special place just for my Prince and me. As I stood in the midst of that garden I would put my hands out to my side and begin to twirl around and around till I would fall to the ground laughing with great joy and delight. Many times that was all the joy I had. As I lay on the ground I would think to myself, "I have to be having more fun than I am supposed to be having.

As I lay there listening to the wind whistling through the trees, the butterflies swirling around my head would make me smile. As I lay there enjoying those moments of peace, I could hear footsteps coming in the distance. My heart would rush at the thought that it was Him, my Prince of Peace, my friend, the one whom I could always trust. He was the One who really did love me and the one I could talk to at any time about anything. I knew I could share all my secrets with Him with no fear of rejection or of Him hurting me.

As He approached my heart pounded with great joy. As He got closer He would stop and call my name with such love in His voice for me. Jumping to my feet and running as fast as I could across that garden with my arms open wide I arrived into His loving arms. As He embraced me, we twirled around and round laughing with such great joy. Such love and joy filled my heart as He held me in His arms again.

He was always dressed in a radiant white robe with a purple sash hanging over His shoulder. His hair was long and brown and a beautiful crown full of jewels sat on His head. His eyes were as blue as the ocean. It was if you could see right through them. They were so piercing that they seemed to look into the depths of my soul. All I ever felt from Him was love and a sense of safety. Somehow I felt like He knew all I was going through, and He felt the pain that I felt.

Many days I would just walk with Him and hold His hand. On the harder days it was just enough to know He was right there beside me. On other days we would sit and talk for hours. At other times we would run, laugh and play. I loved every moment I spent with Him. There were also the silly days of running and twirling around until we were so dizzy we would fall to the ground laughing so hard. When the laughter would stop we would just lie there and watch the clouds roll by. The trees seemed so tall at that moment as the wind rushed through them. Time seemed endless there in that garden where I felt so safe and secure.

I believe the Lord knew me from the foundations of the earth. He knew exactly what I would have to face in my life. He knew the plans He had for me and that the Enemy would try to take me out so I could not accomplish any of those things. He also knew it would take some great intervention on His part to keep me walking with Him. If He did not step into my life when I was little and show me my secret garden of the Most High, I really believe I would not have made it through the pain and sorrow. I know without Him, I would never have found the freedom I walk in today. Why He chose me, I am not really sure but I am thankful He did.

I was that little girl who was lost. He chose to come and dwell with me, and He stayed even after I had locked Him away behind His wall of lattice. He never left me. He just stayed there attending the small portion of my heart where I had left Him. He waited so very patiently for me to come running back into His arms again.

Why not make Him my Prince of Peace, someone to run to when I was afraid? He knew I would be dealing with abandonment, rejection, abuse and many other challenges in my life. He also knew people would have to be put in place to rescue me from situations that were harmful to me. He knew the Enemy would use people to try to destroy my life. The Enemy had it out for me so He gave me a secret place where I could hide under the shadow of the Almighty's wings.

In Psalms 139, it says that my frame was not hidden from Him as I was being formed in the secret places of my mother's womb. I was intricately and curiously wrought as if embroidered with various colors in the depths of the earth, a region of darkness and mystery. His eyes saw my unformed substance and in His book, all my days were written down before they ever took shape when as yet, there was none of them.

God knew I needed a hiding place that I could remember. He knew I would build up those walls to protect myself. He knew my secret garden would become a place where no one was allowed to enter. He knew it would be under lock and key for years. He even knew the day and time I would finally unlock that portion.

Thank God, He decided I was worth waiting for! He knew every detail of my life. The color of my hair and eyes. He chose my chin and my nose. He made my smile, my hands, and my feet. He chose my mom and dad. He wrote all my days down. Did He choose for me to be abandoned by my mom and dad? Did He choose for me to go through all the abuse? I do not believe He wanted any of those things for me.

I do not believe He ever chooses bad for us. I believe we live in a corrupt world and the Enemy uses anything and anyone to try to destroy our lives. I also believe that the sins of our fathers, mothers, and past generations, can cause curses and bad things to be passed on to us unless they are broken. The Bible says the sins of the father will go to the third and fourth generation. Unless those sins are broken and the believer lives a holy and pure life before the Lord, the sins can go on.

My mom and dad divorced because my dad decided to look at another woman as his father had done before him. He probably thought the grass was greener on the other side of the fence. The Enemy wove his way into the lives of my parents and destroyed their marriage. Not only did he tear their marriage apart but he ripped apart three children's lives as well. Now, I can look back and see how the Enemy wanted to destroy me even in my mother's womb.

It is very obvious that the Lord has had His hand upon me from the beginning. Did the Lord intend for me to be abused by my stepfather? No, I believe my mom made a very bad choice because she wanted so much to be loved. She lost her first love to cheating and divorce and all she wanted was someone to make her feel alive and happy again. She chose men who abused her and her children. Was it her fault? Probably, some of it was her fault because of that deep wound she carried in her heart and it was hard for her to make good choices. My mom really did love my dad with all her heart and it hurt her very much to have her family torn apart. She made her choices out of that painful place.

If I had not gone through all the trials I have been through in my life, I would not have found the Lord. I believe He shed tears for the pain I felt. I also would not have the relationship that I have with Him now. Those scars were very deep but my Jesus is bigger than them all. He is my strength and my peace. How great is the depth of His love for us. He will go to great depth to rescue and set us free from the bondage we hold ourselves in.

Like me, you may have abandonment or rejection issues in your life. You may blame the Lord for all your problems and for the pain from the past. The Lord did not tell people to hurt you. They were being used by the Enemy and making ungodly choices. People who abuse others are not walking with the Lord. The Lord is not the abuser.

The Bible says the Enemy roams around like a lion seeking whom he can destroy. It's up to us to seek the truth about who our accuser is. We have to know who we are in the Lord. We cannot live in fear, doubt or unbelief any longer. We must rise up and be healed from the scars that are in our hearts. So we can go forward and do all God has called us to do.

We also seem to forget that God is our loving Father. He is full of compassion and never wants to hurt us. Satan wraps webs of lies in our minds to make us believe God allowed such bad experiences in our lives to punish us or that we deserve to be treated that way. He makes us believe God is penalizing us for something we did wrong. Satan makes us believe God is just sitting back watching all these things and the abusers will never suffer the consequences of their actions. But that is so far from the truth. God is LOVE!

I believe the Lord sheds tears when we get hurt, and He feels our pain. This world is corrupt and there are evil people in it who are used every day to hurt God's children.

It has taken me years to heal from all the scars of the past and to finally understand why the Lord gave me that dream. It was so I would not become bitter and angry towards Him because of what happened to me as a child.

God made the ultimate sacrifice for us when He sent Jesus to die on the cross. He gave all so we could be free to live victorious lives. Believe me; it is worth it to bring all your pain and sorrows to Him. Let Him make your todays better than yesterday and give you hope for the future. Cast all of your cares upon Him for He cares for you.

Isaiah 53: 5-6 says, "He was wounded for our transgressions. He was bruised for our guilt and iniquities; the chastisement (needful to obtain) peace and well-being for us was upon Him, and with the stripes that wounded Him we are healed and made whole."

Oh! The depth of His love that He would lay down His life for you and me. My heart is overwhelmed with His wonderful love.

As I stand in His presence once again in my heart's garden He whispers in my ear "Dance with ME, MY love" We waltz into the sunset of His love that He has poured upon me. My heart fills once again with great joy and love for my King.

Chapter 3

FROZEN MEMORIES

I had so many memories in my heart that were frozen and stuck in a place I thought no one knew about. It was called my dungeon where I stored the hurts and shame I felt. It was a dreadful place I avoided when I entered my heart's garden. I didn't want Jesus to leave me so I hid it and refused to face reality. I assumed no one would ever get in.

I was a grown woman living in the frozen memories that haunted my past. I tried everything to escape but I never could. Those memories played over and over again in my head. I would run to the Lord and beg Him to take the pain away but I never seemed to be totally free. At that time, I did not know I could take every thought captive (Corinthians 10: 5), instead of dwelling on them and letting them bombard my mind.

All the negative words people said to me when I was a child, all the abuse my stepfather made me endure, all the memories of what he made me do and how I felt so dirty inside were piled up in my mind. It was an open door for the Enemy. I tried many times to escape but had no idea what I was doing. I did not understand the scripture that says in Romans 8:1: "There is now no condemnation in Christ Jesus." Many times we exchange parts of our lives to keep those frozen moments. They become the center of our thoughts and bind us from moving forward.

In Luke 9: 59-60, Jesus told His disciples, "Come, leave all behind and follow Me." Each disciple had something he wanted to go back and do before he could commit to the Lord. Likewise, there are many excuses we make not to let go of the hurts in our past. Jesus tells us those who look back are not fit for the kingdom. I believe He means that as long as we hold on to all that stuff, we will never be free.

I was guilty of this as a young Christian. I could not stop looking back at all the pain and hurt I had experienced as a child. There was so much pain in my heart that it was like an uncontainable, huge thorn bush growing wild. Yet, I continued to cry out, and God continued to be faithful. However, again, I kept opening the door for the Enemy with all the negative thoughts I allowed in my heart. I walked around like a broken China doll that no one could fix. The more I searched for truth, the more I longed for healing.

I became like the widow in Luke 18: 1-8 who cried out day and night for justice. The judge finally granted her petition because she just kept coming and asking every day. The Lord is saying that we are never supposed to stop asking and praying for the healing to come. I was desperate to be free and so I petitioned Him daily. Sometimes, several times a day.

I accepted the Lord again when I was seven years old and was baptized when I was ten years old. I rebelled in my teen years and came back to the Lord when I was twenty-one. Throughout my twenties and thirties, I knew I did not want to stay in that state of mind I had been in for so long. I continued to ask for healing. In those days, I read the Word repeatedly.

I believed every word I read, and that is why I continued to press on. I believed the Lord wanted me to be healed, and He wanted me to forgive those who had hurt me. I tried but I did not understand all that was involved. I knew nothing about generational curses. I knew I was possibly bound by generational curses but I had no idea how to remove them from my life. So to fill up those spaces that were hurting, I got involved in whatever was happening at church. I was there every time the doors were open. I also kept busy being a wife and a mother of four children. If I was always active, I felt I could keep those curses in the background of my mind. I did not try to deal with them.

I was a very reserved, quiet person. Depression consumed me most of the time. I tried to hide it but sometimes, it was so overwhelming. My mother and grandmother both suffered from depression all their lives. I wanted to be free of it. I fought it on a daily basis. God gave me a wonderful husband who has always loved me and made me laugh. He also gave me four beautiful children who have blessed my life. If it wasn't for them, the Lord knows, I probably would not have gotten up in the mornings. They gave me the courage to live each day before the Lord healed me.

I knew the Lord was the only one who could set me free. The big problem was that I really did not understand why or from what I wanted freedom. I just knew something was really wrong in my heart. I felt like Humpty Dumpty who was all broken inside with no one to help put me back together again. I sought people I thought could help me find my way but in the end, I always felt judged and condemned. No one understood me, and no one knew how to help me find that peace I so longed for.

Those frozen places of pain and hurt caused me to make some really bad choices in my life. Out of the fear of rejection, I ran from people who tried to help. Also, I attached myself to people who would just use me and then criticize me behind my back. Some Christians who probably meant well, hurt me terribly with their words. In those days, I had no boldness to stand up for myself. I was so afraid of having a voice back then. I allowed people to walk all over me. I let them speak to me in such bad ways. I could not stand up because I lived in fear of rejection. I think people saw me as weak, and they used me to get whatever they needed done. I allowed it because I wanted to be accepted.

My husband witnessed all the anger and bitterness I felt. I constantly rehashed it over and over again what I should have done or said to those who were doing the damage. I lived it over and over in my mind. I had no rest at night! This continually added to the pain and hurt I felt in my heart.

Although I tried not to carry that pain, it only added to the walls that I built up to protect myself. I longed to be accepted by the Christian community but always felt like an outcast. It seemed like the more I tried to do things their way, the more I felt rejected. Sometimes, Christians can be the cruelest people of all. I am not sure where the, "Love your neighbor as yourself" fits in with all I have been through in the church.

Finally, I realized I needed help but I thought it might have been too late for me. However, God had other plans for my life. I believe His Word! I had read the Word enough by this time to know that every person God puts in our paths is there for a reason. I also believe the roads we find ourselves on and the seasons we are in are answers to prayers we have prayed. Sometimes, we wonder how we arrived at this place or question why God would take us this way. Many times, we have to be put on a road that leads to Him. It may be a very hard road but when we look back, we will truly see it was worth it.

That is what happened to me when the Lord took me on a journey of healing. I had to go on a road of cliffs and mountains to be truly set free from all the frozen places that kept me bound. I had to learn to surrender to His will and not mine. The climb up those hills was very hard and the mountains were extremely steep. At times, I could barely see a foot in front of me. I had to trust Him to guide me through those unknown places. It seemed as if the road would never end. I wanted to move ahead so I would rush thinking all was well, only to have to go back and do it again. I had to stay on that potter's wheel and allow Him to mold and make me into the woman He desires me to be.

I loved singing one of my favorite songs to the Lord during these times: "Change my Heart Oh God." The song says:

> Change my heart, oh God, make it
> ever true.

Change my heart, oh God, let me be
like you.

You are the potter and I am the clay.

Mold me and make me.

This is what I pray.

Change my heart, oh God.

Make it ever true.

Change my heart, oh God.

May I be like you.

By Eddie Espinosa

I love that song because it says everything I have always desired since I was old enough to accept Him.

Many times, I wanted to just quit but the Lord was always right there saying to me, "You can do this; I will give you strength for the journey." When I surrendered, He would pick me up and we would continue the journey together. I finally realized that He was going to be faithful to me. He started this work in me, and He was going to finish what

He started. I realized He was not like man who had left me by the roadside saying I was not worth fixing. I was not pretty enough or perfect like most Christians thought I was supposed to be. They thought I should just get over all the memories and move on. No, He thought I was worth fixing! He poured His time and His love upon me and for this, I am very thankful.

At times, He would send certain people on my path who were truly called by Him. He sent them to help me along this journey. I had to learn how to discern those who were of God and those who were there for their own gain. This became so hard at times because I desperately wanted to be accepted. I had to realize that if He sent people to help, I must be willing to accept and act on what they were speaking into my life. One of the first people He sent in my life is still a part of who I am. I met her when I was very young in the Lord. Her name is Donna Peters. She has taught me so much about standing and believing in all God has called me to do. She has taught me how to forgive by the example she has lived before me. She has taught me how to love people without conditions. I am deeply grateful to the Lord for bringing my spiritual momma into my life. She has truly lived the life of being a teacher to the young.

Nevertheless, when all was said and done, I had to let the Lord heal those broken, frozen places, allowing Him to take those thoughts captive.

It was not an easy path to walk on; however, the more I allowed Him to heal those frozen places in my heart, the more healing I desired. We cannot achieve the fullness of God's future for our lives when pieces of our past continue to consume us. The Word says in Luke 10: 27 that we are to love the Lord our God with all our hearts, minds, and souls and with all our strength. If we are haunted by our past, then we surely cannot love Him with everything. We cannot genuinely know the fullness of His love for us if we are consumed with the past.

We make choices every day; one of those choices must be to surrender to His will for our lives. His love will consume us and then overflow onto others if we allow Him in our lives. There is nothing more powerful than the love the Lord has for each of us that gives peace and joy. When we get to that place, nothing can hold us back from accomplishing all He desires us to do. We have to lay at the altar daily. When we do this we are empowered to go out and preach, teach, pray for others and lay hands on the sick so they will recover as it says in Mark 16:15-20. God did not put us here to warm pews in churches or to just be about our gain. No, He created us to live our lives for Him. We are to worship Him by our actions and our words daily.

The Night the Prophet Spoke to Me

My journey to the point when true healing began had already been long and hard, but I continued on the road to which He called me. The major journey began on a hot summer's evening in August the year I turned forty. A good friend of mine invited me to attend a meeting where a prophet was speaking. I was very guarded and skeptical at that time. For me to even be at this meeting was a miracle. I knew the Bible talked about prophecy but I really had never experienced any of it in my life.

As I sat in that service and listened to this man of God speak, I was intrigued but still uncertain. It just didn't seem real to me. We were not even in a church but in a small store. I almost felt as if it was a scene from a movie where we were trying to hide something. The man spoke about all his journeys and all the amazing things the Lord had done. It was a small meeting and at the end of the service, he offered to pray for people. My friend encouraged me to go forward, and I went to the end of the line. I started to pray as I listened to him pray for the other people. He was casting out some deep stuff in their lives. I got a little scared as to what he might say to me so I began to pray harder. I said to the Lord, "This is the deal; this man had better say something to me that only you and I know or I will never believe a word he says."

Little did I know when I stepped up there to be prayed for that the Lord would use this man to speak things into my life that would change me forever. This first encounter of the prophetic led me to others the Lord used to speak change and freedom into my life. It took several years for me to walk in total freedom but from that first moment, I knew something had changed inside me.

When I stepped forward, the tears flowed so quickly I could not control them. That servant of God who stood before me began to cry when he looked into my eyes. I knew at that moment God was in the room. The man said to me, "I see a little girl in a corner of a basement, and she is weeping and crying uncontrollably. Her lips are quivering and she is so fearful. She is curled up in a small ball as if to hide from someone. Her legs are bleeding because she has been beaten so badly. That little girl is you, right? And you know who did this to you."

I answered, "yes" through all my tears. God had reached down so deep inside me to reveal such a memory that I never wanted to remember. He then began to tell me how I had all these things hanging around my neck. They were the generational curses that had been passed on and on: depression, oppression, sickness, poverty and so many others. The prophet said they were like huge cow bells hanging around my neck, holding me down. He began to rebuke the devourer off my life and all the things that had oppressed me for so long.

When he was done, I felt like a ton of bricks had lifted off my shoulders. I could not even talk. I went home with such great peace inside that I could not even explain it. Healing began that night. However, I had to choose to walk on that road of peace and not pick all that stuff up again. I could not allow the Enemy to take back the ground the Lord had restored. It was truly a war for my life and my soul.

For two years, I was OK but struggled sometimes. I knew there had to be more but had no idea how to find it. I was attending a church where not much was going on, except people warming pews and being part of a social club. I wanted more than that in my life. When I saw the homeless being bused in, I thought, "OK, finally, something is changing." But it was all for show. The homeless were made to sit in the very back row sectioned off from everyone else. Before the altar call was made, they were taken outside, given a sack lunch, put back on the bus and returned to the streets. It broke my heart when I asked why and the reply was, "We have to do it that way."

It was not long after that our son told us about a church he had started attending. He kept saying, "Mom, this is the church that is doing everything it says in the Word we are supposed to do." At first, I did not believe him because I had seen so much. After a few weeks, we decided to visit the church. We walked in to see all these homeless people being a part of the service, not sitting in the back row. We were truly amazed at what we saw. This church was living what the Word says in Mark 16. We never went back to the other church. It was by God's design that we ended up at the new church. The Lord used many people in that place to speak healing and freedom into my life.

Carpet Time

I spent many Sunday mornings at the altar seeking more healing. Every time the Holy Spirit said, "Go get prayed for," I went. I did not want to leave any stone undone. God was always faithful to show up each time I surrendered to Him. I spent a lot of time slain in the Spirit. I called that "carpet time" because it was always happening. I learned to yield to His Spirit and just knew there must be a reason. I know many people thought it was an act but it was not. I truly was being healed in those moments, in that stillness with the Lord.

The first few times it happened, I would lay there for a few seconds, resist, and get up. I began to learn that God was healing me as I yielded to His precious Holy Spirit. He was doing a great work in my heart as I lay in His presence. The more I yielded, the more He healed me, so I was in no rush to get up. Sometimes, if I tried to and the Lord was not done with me, He would put me right back down as if He was saying, "Now trust Me. Trust Me to release you when I am finished working in the area of your heart that needs healing." At other times, laughter would just overwhelm me; I could not stop laughing. Laughter is very healing.

Many times, I would still be laying on that floor when all had left the sanctuary, but I did not even care. I just wanted to be in His presence until He said it was time to go. I was on a mission to know Him, and I treasured each time He allowed me to be with Him. I wanted to be free and that was all that really mattered to me. I did not care who understood anymore or even if they laughed at me behind my back, which some probably did. They went on with their lunches and all they had to do while I just lay in His presence. I would not change one of those moments with Him. I learned so much, especially how to know when He walks into the room.

He taught me how to be in His presence and worship Him with a pure heart, and I would not trade that for anything. The things He deposited in my heart in those moments have been life-changing. It is because of those moments I can go before Him any time I choose and know He will listen to me and my prayers. He taught me how to hear His voice and to know how to discern it from the others. So many things were poured into me in my "carpet time." Some of them are mine to just keep in my heart and not share with anyone. This is why I can say that I waltz with Him because He has given me so very much. He has given me pearls of gold no one can ever take from me. I know in those moments, He was right beside me pouring His heart into mine. He was filling me with such great love for Him and His people because He knew He had called me to do a great work for Him. Often, people get slain in the Spirit but do not wait because of fear of what man thinks. Trust me, I lived all that once upon a time, and I am very thankful I learned to surrender and give Him freedom in my life.

I had always been a worshiper but now, I worship even more. I found my peace in worship. As I shut everyone else out, I see my King. In those moments, I would be in His arms and we would waltz. Peace and joy would always flood my soul. Yes, I was judged because many thought I was too out there. I was told, "Do not sing because your voice is not pretty enough." God would say to me, "Do not listen to them; they are about perfection. I am about what is in your heart."

Singing in the Spirit

It hurt so badly when they said these things but the Lord would gently wrap me in His arms and say, "Sing to Me." I have also been told by many that I have a beautiful voice. Truth is all I know is I love to sing and I sing from my heart, not from perfection. It is because I sing from my heart that I learned to yield to the Holy Spirit and started singing in the Spirit years before many were doing it in the church. I could hear the words to the songs in my spirit and then I would sing them.

At one point, I was going to sing a special. When I told the song leader what I wanted to sing and how I was going to sing it in the Spirit as the Lord led, she became angry and argued with me. She informed me it was not possible to do that. I argued that I could, and she took me before the pastor's. I was told by them also that it could not be done and my desire was from the Enemy. I tried to explain but they were always right, and I was always wrong.

I walked out in tears that night and wanted to leave the church but God would not let me. He told me it was ignorance on their parts because they had never experienced such. He also said I was experiencing things in worship before the church was. They were behind and they did not understand and so, I needed to forgive them for their ignorance. Still, it was hard because I was laughed at behind my back and whispered about. They said I was not a good enough speaker and other things. Though they hurt me, I kept forgiving and taking their cruel punishment.

I am thankful I went through all that now and I did not stop singing in the Spirit. The Word says to pray in the Spirit at all times and to sing in the Spirit songs of praise. Now, I do not care what people think. I refuse to allow a man to tell me that I cannot worship my Lord in songs of the Spirit. I do not care if they do not like my voice; I just love on my Lord. That is what we are supposed to do.

I found out that there is nothing in my past that is worth keeping me from my Lord. Finally, I also discovered that nothing my past is as important as what God has planned for me and my future.

Healing at Esther's House

After many, many hours of carpet time, the Lord led me to another period of healing. This time of healing was different from what I had ever experienced in my life. The ministry is based on the book of Esther. It is a place for women in leadership to attend. There, I was able to get away and find who I was again and be revived. The first group I was in had eight women.

I stayed in a beautiful Victorian home in Butler, Mo. While I was there, I was asked not to leave the home for that period of time so the Holy Spirit's presence would not be quenched. It was the most wonderful experience in my life. I was treated like a queen, which I had never experienced in my life. I was waited on and not allowed to do anything for myself except spend time in the Lord's presence. This was a precious time for me with the Lord. When my sisters in the Lord washed my feet, I cried and cried because I had always felt so unworthy to ever be treated with love. I always thought I was ugly but there, I felt beautiful in every way. My experiences there changed my life forever.

The Lord set me up for a woman of God to speak into my life what needed to be said to me. It was done with such love that it pierced my heart. When she asked me to step into the place of prayer, she began telling me that as a little girl my innocence had been stolen from me. And it caused me to be locked in the emotions of that little girl. I had grown up physically but in my heart, I had stayed trapped as that child. She also said many people thought that the Lord should just spank me and tell me to get over it. But He had known me from childhood, and He knew how hard it was for me to let it all go. He reassured me in those moments that it would all be okay. He knew I could not handle any brash handling. That is why He took His time healing me slowly.

She said I had even locked the Lord up behind a wall of lattice because I had found Him as a child. I was afraid that He would run from me because of the ugliness I felt inside. I felt dirty and unclean before Him. She began to tell me about His eyes peering through that lattice. She said that is what caught my eyes. It was those beautiful eyes that had pierced my soul so long ago. She told me it was okay to unlock that door now and allow the Lord to come out. I could trust that He would leap over the hills and stand upon the mountains with me. Those hills were the things I feared would turn into mountains. She asked me to give Him the keys to my heart where I had locked Him away.

I surrendered with many tears and on my face, slain in the Spirit, lying at His feet. When I got up off that floor, I sat in His presence for what seemed like hours. He spoke so many things to me. That evening, as we began to worship, I closed my eyes to see Him there. He said to me, "Come dance with Me, My love." He beckoned me to come so I yielded to Him and began a beautiful waltz of love with my Prince. As He carried me around that room I was in His arms, and there was no one else there. I looked into those beautiful eyes that had rescued me and fell in love with my Prince all over again. I was finally in His arms.

I returned home with hope and many words from the Lord. But the mountain I had just climbed would lead to another valley of trials and testing. However, I knew I could dance with Him any time I desired because I had finally let Him out from behind those walls.

Psalms 23 and Matthew 6: 33-34 became my life scriptures. I poured myself into the Word and in prayer and learned more and more about God. My soul yearned for His presence and my heart waited for Him, the Lover of my soul. My heart flooded with great joy again as He beckoned me to come dance with Him. As we embraced we again waltzed throughout the garden. I knew I would be able to feel His loving arms surround me forever.

Chapter 4

HEAVEN'S RAIN

Jesus, the rain of heaven, stepped back into my life on that warm beautiful summer's day. That moment will be locked in my memories forever. Time had stood still in those places where my emotions were on lockdown.

Our hearts are like many gardens that all become one as we become one with the Lord. We choose to let them grow into a place where there is only peace, joy, and love or we can allow them to be gardens filled with bitterness, hatred, and unforgiveness. We make the choice about what to do with those memories of our past.

Changed but Still Broken

I may have been a grown woman but inside I felt like a little girl who did not know how to control her emotions. I had lost so much that I wondered how I would ever be able to recapture any of my hopes or dreams. After my healing at the Victorian home, I went home to the same old routine. I was changed but still broken. Jesus would have to take me on many roads ahead for me to finally find His peace.

I wanted so much to feel like His queen in His arms again, but I still struggled with the past. I was still trapped inside an emotional roller coaster full of fear, doubt, and unbelief most of the time. Sometimes, for no reason at all, my entire mind would fill with anger and rage. I would explode in a fit like a child who did not get her way. I would run out of my house, get into my car and just drive anywhere. I would sit in that car and cry relentlessly. Sometimes, that lasted for hours and other times for only a while. I would pray and talk to the Lord asking why it kept happening to me.

I had this great misconception that all the healing was over but it really had only just begun. I finally stopped running and woke up to the realization that this was only the beginning. I had to seriously look at my heart and what I saw was not a pretty picture. In retrospect, I am thankful the Lord really took His time with me. I know now that even though I wanted to be healed, I probably could not have handled it all at once.

Every step of the process of healing those broken places has been one of pain and love intermingled. Every root of anger, bitterness, and unforgiveness had to be uprooted and replanted with love, joy, and peace. Each step of surrender became a step of faith and trust for me. Every step has led me to a much closer walk with Him.

My Prince of Peace was able to rain down and take this spiritual journey with me. Freedom came with every step I took to search for His truth and let Him uproot the old ways of thinking, and plant new thoughts of hope and peace in my heart. Each time I stepped into those places of fear, doubt, and unbelief I had to let the rain of heaven fall on me. My faith grew and hope was resurrected. I would let go of fear and replace it with trust. Finally, at times, I could say, "It is well with my soul."

It Is What We Choose to Do that Really Matters.

The process of emotional healing is not an easy road to walk on but it is a road that most of us must travel at some point in our lives. It is what we choose to do that really matters. We all have pain and hurt from our past. If you say you don't have any, praise God but you are probably in the minority. Some people are just able to lay it all down, walk away and never have any scars. For me, however, the scars were really too deep to just walk away.

I am sure there are many out there walking around with painful scars no one knows about. These are the ones my heart longs to help. I want to give you a big hug and tell you how much the Lord loves you. I want you to know that you are beautiful in His eyes and no matter how you feel inside, you can be healed and have great peace.

We build walls to protect ourselves so we do not get hurt again. The problem is that we end up hurting ourselves without even knowing it. As wall after wall goes up, we seem to think its okay because we are protecting ourselves.

You may have started building the walls in your childhood like most of us do, especially if we have been hurt. He will take all those places that were broken and fill them up with His love and compassion. Also, you may have never been taught how to forgive those who hurt you. But the Prince of Peace can take all those places that are broken and mend them with His love and compassion He is so gracious to take us by the hand even when we are grown up and lead us through those hurtful places. I found my heart being filled with love, joy and peace. All those seeds of bitterness towards the ones who had hurt me in the past were taken out and filled with compassion for them. That is what He longs to do in each of our hearts.

I always thought no one knew the pain I felt, but the Lord knew and longed to set me free. He is the only one that could have ever stepped into all the broken places one step at a time and brought complete and total healing in my life. He left no stone unturned. If I had not allowed His healing rain in my life so long ago, I would have never known His love and peace the way I do today. I would never have known that such peace could be achieved. I would have remained that emotional little girl trapped forever. That was the day my Prince of Peace stepped out of His bondage that I had created and into my garden again. I stood there in the midst seeing nothing but gates, bars and darkness everywhere. It was like there had been a terrible war there.

It took time but as I allowed Him to unlock each place then I finally began to see life come back into my heart and myself. It became an awesome adventure each time I would go spend time with Him. I watched Him overflow my life and change me from a broken woman to a healed one.

As I close my eyes now and whisper His name, I am there in the midst of that beautiful place He has created for me. I stand waiting for my Prince of Peace to come and sit with me awhile. I look around and see nothing but beauty. There are no more broken places to fix. Yes, I will still have mountains to climb but I can truly say all is well with my soul.

Like me, you can learn how to live Proverbs 3: 5-6. I trust only in Him, not my own understanding. I do not know the way to go but He certainly does. I can look around and see all the love He has poured into me to restore all the Enemy stole from me. I stand with my arms outstretched to the sides looking up towards the heavens as the sun pours down on me. His joy floods my soul as the rain of heaven falls like a mist around me, and a rainbow of love appears before me. I can truly say now that all His promises are true.

When I look in the mirror today I no longer see that little girl who was so broken inside. I no longer see the little girl who saw herself as fat and ugly and thought no one would ever love her. No, now, I see a beautiful woman who is complete on the inside and loved by the King of Kings Himself. That day finally came when I realized that my Prince had truly ridden in on his white stallion and rescued me. He did not leave me back in those places. He conquered them all.

If I could have done anything differently, it would have been to open my heart sooner and release Him from that locked up place where I kept Him. The road I chose has not been easy but every step of healing has been worth it.

When we choose to walk with the Lord, we are not always understood. But are we supposed to be understood? God called us to be in the world but not to be conformed to it. I have always been different from others and even called peculiar. I am fine with that now because I am different. I am the daughter of the Most High God and no one can ever take that from me again. I will stand up for the Word of God anytime I am given the chance, and I will defend my Lord.

For too long the Enemy had me under lock and key through fear. I was so fearful to stand, share or sing but I am no longer afraid because I know that Jehovah Sabbaoth stands beside me along with legions of angels. God did not give me a spirit of fear but He gave me a sound mind. Every time He provides a platform to share I will share whatever He says. I am obedient to Him, for He is my Lord and Savior.

I knew a long time ago the Lord was calling me to do a new and different thing in my life for Him. I searched very long for someone who understood how to help me be the leader God wanted me to be. I dealt with so many who held me back because they could never see what God wanted me to do.

They saw me only behind the scenes but I have always known God called me to be a leader.

There have been others who have been judgmental and bitter towards me because God put me in a position they thought I should never have. Many have been jealous of all God has done for me. I know these things because the Lord showed me. The closer you get to the Lord, the more He shares. I have learned to rest and wait until He opens the door for me. I am in a place where He is teaching me how to just trust Him for everything. I have committed to pressing on to His higher calling because He will not let me quit and because I have come too far now to ever quit.

It burns in my heart to share what my Lord has done in my life with all people everywhere who are broken and hurting. Everyone needs hope and to know that there is life after abuse and rejection. He is the only one who can take a broken mess and heal our hearts so completely that we can rest. We are the only ones who ever stand in the way of being healed by God. He longs to make a place in our hearts where we can come and just talk with Him without shame. He loves each of us and longs to be our guidance director if we let Him. It is in this place we will be forever free.

This is a place of peace and rest where, if a storm comes in our lives and the sea gets bumpy, we already know He has us in His loving arms. This is a place where at times, we can leave the cares of this world behind and lay them at His feet. We can walk in a place where we are totally relying and leaning on Him in that peace. This is a place where we run into His arms; He embraces us and whispers in our ears, "Come dance with Me, My love."

The Prince of Peace longs to shine and rain down His love and promises of healing upon you. When He steps into your heart's garden, He will illuminate every area in your heart that has been hurt and broken. As He begins to shine upon those areas, you will become alive again. Your eyes will open to His love, and peace; joy will flood your soul. Then you will see all the hidden walls that you have built to keep Him out. You will see how they have consumed your entire life. Most of all, you will see the truth of who you really are.

When you see who you really are, you will fall on your face at His feet crying for mercy. Then the Prince of Peace will take your hands in His and help you to your feet. He will wipe your tears and embrace you with His love. As you look into those beautiful eyes that have once again pierced your soul, your heart's garden will overflow with great joy, and you will finally know that Heaven's rain has stepped into your heart's garden to heal all the places that were broken.

He then takes you into His arms again as He gently kisses you on your forehead and whispers in your ear, "My child, I love you, and My healing rain is here. There is nothing more to fear!" As His light floods your heart's garden, you begin your journey of waltzing through those healing roads ahead.

Chapter 5

THE RUINS

After allowing the Lord out from behind His wall of lattice. I thought that all was complete. I still had a lot to learn about how the Lord even operates. He finally had access to my life again, but I still had all these hidden areas.

Being a grown woman and having the emotions of a seven year old was very difficult at times. I had been through so much in my life with my health and emotions that I was desperate to see some real change. I had to become the willing vessel in the potter's hands again.

Though the Lord had begun to bring some relief from the depression and oppression, I still would fall back into that trap because I would open up the door. My mind constantly fed me doubt and unbelief. I always made a choice to put myself there instead of trusting the Lord.

I felt so much anger inside, because I had received from the Lord so much already but felt like I was throwing some of it away. I did not know how to claim the word and stand on it at that point. I sat down one day and decided I was tired of running from who I was really supposed to be. I needed to see what the Lord saw.

As I began to examine my heart, I found myself standing on this very small patch of ground. As I looked around I saw walls and walls surrounding that small patch of ground. There were gates and locks on each wall. My dungeon was completely hidden from view.

My garden that was once so beautiful when I was a child was now this terrible place of ruins, except for that very small patch of ground. I wondered how I had come to this place in my life. I looked around for my Prince of Peace who had always been there for me. I called out His name and He called back to me. I turned to see Him behind that wall of lattice peering through. I had given Him the key but I had kept the wall up. He beckoned me to come in to that small portion of the garden I had left for Him. As I walked in I fell on my knees before crying. I was consumed with grief for I was the one who had built all these walls up not Him.

Through many tears of repentance I promised Him I would give Him every key to every gate in my garden, I even committed to give Him access to my dungeon at some point. He took me in His arms and assured me that I could trust Him. I melted at His feet as I surrendered all the keys of my heart to Him forever. I had to trust Him to choose how we would go to those walls and when.

His portion of my heart's garden had not changed from when I was a child. It still had the beautiful wild flowers of blue, yellow and purple. It still had all the beautiful roses growing there. He had been there all along just waiting on me to come back to my first love. He reassured me that all of my heart's garden would someday look the same as this.

I stood there looking around because I was in no rush that day. I wanted to just breathe it all in. In one corner there was a waterfall and a huge tree with a swing on it. I remembered swinging on it when I was a little girl. I remembered talking with my Prince there. Those were such vivid memories coming back to me. I started crying knowing that I had locked all of them away. He took my hands in His and assured me it would be okay.

He patiently waited for me to trust him again. Together we went into each area and He conquered all my fears. He taught me how to abide under the shadow of His wings.

I was so happy on the inside, because I had finally found Him again. On the outside though I was an emotional basket case. I continued to shut most people out of my life except a few friends and my family. As time went on I wanted more of my heart to be healed. I began to search and long to know Him more. Not only as my Savior and the lover of my soul, but also as my friend. I finally knew in my heart that I was never going to just be another person who called herself Christian and not having a personal relationship with Him. I longed for so much more. I wanted to know this one who loved me so much when I did not even deserve to be loved by Him.

Many people stayed away from me because they saw me as an emotional mess. They did not know or even care about all the emotional scars that I carried. Some people have this misconception that if we are saved that we are healed. We are healed if we know how to release it to the Lord, but most of us are not healed from emotional scars that way. It is a process of time. Those emotional scars were forming my thoughts and actions.

On the outside I was a true mess. I was depressed, oppressed, angry, withdrawn and downcast. I felt very unwanted and unworthy of any love. I saw myself as ugly and unloved every day of my life. I rarely believed it when people would say they loved me. I still lived with the torment daily of being rejected. Fear, doubt and unbelief consumed me. I also lived with the fear that if I did not do enough for people that they would not love me. That included my husband and my children. I was still so angry inside over all I had been through. I felt like I had lost something, and I did not know how to ever get it back.

There was this war going on inside me, and I had no idea how to control it anymore. The more I hungered to know the lord, the more the war raged inside for change. What kept pushing me forward is the fact that I no longer wanted to be the old me. I wanted so much to be like my Prince of Peace.

The more I surrendered to His will the more peace would come.

Surrendering our will to His can be very difficult at times. However if we desire change in our lives, we have to learn how to surrender to Him and His will for us. The more I surrendered to Him, the more I changed on the inside, because the inside that was all broken was beginning to be put back together piece by piece.

Even though I was really misunderstood by the Christian world the Lord understood me. He took His time healing me because He knew exactly how fragile I was. He was not going to rush me through those areas and risk me locking Him back behind that wall and me giving up. He knew I had been judged and condemned by the Christian world enough. He knew I would have ran away from Him if He would have treated me the way they thought He should have. No, He loved me more than man could ever imagine.

So He took His sweet loving time healing my emotional scars. He did not care what anyone thought about how He chose to do it. He did it His loving way and I am so thankful. He knew how deep those scars ran in me and He knew all the roots of lies the enemy had planted in me. He went the extra mile for me because I was worth it.

Many times I would make an effort with my own strength to work on those broken places. I would try so hard to release them to Him, but would never find peace. It seemed that ugly dungeon area that I feared the most would always raise its head, putting me in fear to surrender to the Lord. On those days that I would fail I would run into His arms asking Him to not make me go to that place of hurt.

The Lord was so good to me. Every attempt I would make He would cheer me on. He was so patient and loving with me. Always waiting till I was ready to try again. Matt 6:33 Says seek Him first and His righteousness. I had to learn how to do that, and sometimes it was easy and others it was not.

When I went to the gathering at Esther's house the first time the Lord used a wonderful servant of His, Dr. Joyce Wallace, to speak into my life to explain to me about how I would learn to trust the Lord again. In those first moments of learning to trust Him it was so very hard, because I had to learn how to swim in those rivers of trust again. Those rivers that flow from the springs of life that surround God's throne. Ezekiel tells about how the angel measured out a cubit of water and it was up to my ankles, then I trusted Him a little because I was still in control of everything. Then it says the angel measured out another cubit of water and it was up to my knees; but I was still in control, so I trusted a little bit more. Then it says the angel measured out another cubit of water, and it was up to my waist. Then it became harder to trust Him, but I learned how to walk and trust Him even more in the midst of those waters. Then it says the angel of the Lord measured out another cubit of water and it was up to my shoulders, so I had to swim in that river of trust with Him. I learned how to take His hand in mine and swim in that river of life's circumstances. After some time went by, I learned how to trust Him completely and we began to work together on all the broken areas. It was different now because I no longer tried to do it all on my own. My Prince of Peace walked right beside me through all the broken places in my heart. He brought peace and rest with every step we took together.

Chapter 6

THE RUINS - MY DAD

The first troubling area of my life the Lord wanted me to work on was my dad. During the healing process, there always seemed to be a class the Lord would lead me to. He would use the teaching in that class to open my eyes and show me things I had not seen before.

I attended a class called "The Grace Class" which I went to at my friend's request. I sat in that class the first night and listened to David Baldwin teach on how we build up walls in our hearts. I was amazed.

It was as if God had told this man something about me. At one point in the class he said, "I want you to just stop and examine your heart for a time here, and then I want you to write down who the Lord brings before you." I sat there praying and listening to the Lord. I knew in my heart He wanted me to resolve issues about my dad.

As I sat there in those moments, I realized I had several feelings about my dad locked up behind a huge brick wall. Although by this time in my life I had built a semi-relationship with my dad, I was not willing to open up to him and allow him to know the real me. I kept him at a distance because he had abandoned me once, and I was afraid he would do it again. I really had a lot of fear about opening up that door. I think I was scared to face those painful memories of my childhood. I also really did not know what true forgiveness looked like.

I think sometimes when we get hurt as children by those who are supposed to protect and love us, we think they need to feel our pain. We get the victim mentally. We grow up thinking it is okay not to forgive them because they hurt us. We even think its okay to be angry at them but it's really not. Most of the time, the person we are holding captive by our anger or unforgiveness is unaware they have hurt us or even done anything wrong.

When I look back at that thick brick wall I had put up against my dad, I wonder how I ever opened up my heart to let him in my life. He always said he never wanted me and it became one of his excuses for leaving my mom when she was pregnant with me. I do not remember him ever being a meaningful part of my life so for me to even allow him in was a true miracle.

For some reason, I always wanted to know him even though all I ever heard my mother say about him was negative. My grandparents said very little about him. At age eighteen, I made a huge decision to call my dad to try building our relationship. I needed to understand why he had left me and if it was my fault. I really wanted to know, be loved, and accepted by my daddy. By this time in my life,

I had my daughter and was thinking how I would explain to her someday that her daddy had abandoned her like mine had done to me.

I think all little girls look up to their daddy's as their heroes. He is supposed to be there when you fall down and get hurt. And to save you from the scary things that might be under your bed. He is expected to tuck you in at night, give you sweet kisses, and always tell you he loves you. To carry you on his shoulders and help you ride your first bike. To teach you to roller skate and to have silly tea parties with you. He is supposed to be there on your first day of school and all the programs. To be proud of you and who you become. To be there on your first date as that young man comes to pick you up. He is supposed to approve the man you have chosen to marry and then walk you down the aisle when you get married.

These are things I could only dream about with my dad because he was never there for me or my brothers. Even after I let him in my life, he really never took part the way I wanted him to. I probably expected more than he knew how to give or even wanted to give. He really did not know me that well. From the moment I was old enough to remember, my mom was filling my head with hateful words about my dad. I understand now why she did it. However back then, I did not.

I always dreamed of my daddy rescuing me from all the monsters that surrounded me every day of my life. To me, it was only a dream because he would never get the chance to do any of those things I dreamed of. I would face each day growing up thinking my dad did not want me. I really wanted love and acceptance more than anything.

My dad has always had a cruel sense of humor, and he always seemed to say something about my weight or what I did or said — that really hurt. Not that he meant to hurt me — but he always did. I was already very sensitive about myself anyway, but it seemed like he picked on those things on purpose. So I kept him at a safe distance.

Because my dad was not there for me when I was little, my grandpa stepped in to try and fill his shoes. I knew he always loved and accepted me. Was it my dad's fault that I felt the way I did? I am not sure he even knew what I was thinking or how I even felt because I was always too afraid to tell him. Some of his choices were part of it I am sure but I also believe that my mom had something to do with the choices my dad made about me.

During the class, the Lord reminded me that at about four years old, my dad came to pick up my brothers. My stepmom was in the car and when they drove in, my mom rushed out and the two of them began to argue. I was standing in the yard watching this entire argument take place. My dad told my brothers to get in the car. I said, "Daddy I want to go with you." He said, "No you cannot go because your mom will not let you." I began to cry! As my brothers got in the car, my mom and stepmom were still exchanging words. As they drove off, my mom grabbed me and pulled me in the house while I was screaming and crying, "I want my daddy!" over and over again. My mom started screaming at me to shut up and then yelled that I would never see my daddy again.

In some ways, she was right because it was five years before I remember seeing him again. By that time, I did not even remember what he looked like, so I did not recognize him when I saw him. Also, my mom had left me for good at my grandparents' home to live. She had moved across the country to California. I will never forget that memory of meeting my dad and not even knowing it was him.

My grandparents had taken me to a grand opening of a new store. The store was very crowded and there was a storm going on outside. My grandpa wanted to get out of there because the tornado sirens were going off. People were trying to leave but the police officers were closing off the doors. People were pushing and shoving, and then the lights went out. My grandpa grabbed my grandma's hand and mine and said, "Let's go to the back of the store were the automotive department is and see if we can get out."

As we approached that area, they saw this man who came up to them and shook my grandpa's hand. My grandma gave him a hug. They started talking to him like they knew him really well. I was so scared of the storm that I just hid behind my grandma. My grandpa told me to go out and sit on the bench in the garage area and wait for him to bring the car in. So I went and sat down. I kept wondering who that man was but I did not ask. As I sat there, the man kept talking to my grandma then he came over to me and stooped down and said, "Hi." I was surprised that he knew my name. He asked me how I was and some other questions but I just sat there shaking because I was so scared of the storm on the outside.

When my grandpa drove in with the car, I climbed in the back seat. The man told me goodbye. When we drove off, I leaned forward and asked my grandparents "Who was that man you were talking to?"

They said, "You should know who he is."

I said, "No, who is he?"

Then they said, "That is your daddy!"

I was totally amazed that I had met my daddy and did not even know him. After that, my grandpa started taking me over to see my dad about every six months but I really was never allowed to spend any time with him.

That wall I had built in my heart was very thick. It was a wall of deep rejection and abandonment from the womb. As said earlier, before I was born, my dad separated from my mom and divorced her when I was one. Then he remarried when I was two. Growing up in all that bitterness and almost hatred that my mom had for him was very confusing as a little girl. I was not sure whether to like him or hate him like she did.

I can remember my mom always saying to me even as an adult, "What are you going to do? Go call your daddy to come rescue you?" It was never nice when she said that. It would pierce my heart over and over as she spoke about him so negatively. I knew he was not perfect but deep inside, I really wanted him to love me. Finally, when I started seeing my dad at eighteen, it caused my mom so many issues because of all the unforgiveness in her heart. She was extremely jealous on her part too. Most of the time, I had to ignore what she was saying because I had chosen not to base my relationship with my dad upon anything she said anymore.

So on that night in that class I sat there writing out some of those memories; I went home to have even more come. I chose to open up my heart and receive all the Lord wanted to give me. The Lord drew me to that wall and began to show me the things I had held in my heart and why I built up the wall in the first place

As I stepped into that area of my heart again after all those years, all I could see were weeds as tall as me. Nothing beautiful grew there! It was so dark and hopeless. I fell on my face at His feet and began to cry, asking Him to forgive me for not allowing Him in this area sooner. He knelt down beside me, and with His loving arms around me, said, "You are forgiven." The more I stayed in that place the more healing came. The Lord began to tear down the weeds, which were lies and the deception the Enemy had planted in my heart about my dad. Floods of the Lord's presence poured over me, and I began the surrendering process. After many times of going there with the Lord, I was finally able to surrender all those things that hurt so deeply to the Lord.

I finally realized that it was the Lord who had brought my dad and me back together. He showed me how He had given me another chance to know my dad and that he could restore what the Enemy had stolen from me. He truly is the restorer of relationships. He had heard my heart's cry from a young girl. He knew I wanted to know my daddy. He gave me back what was stolen from me so long ago.

The Lord replaced all that pain I felt about my dad with love and compassion. I can finally look back on my childhood and not feel pain about my dad's absence. Yes, it is still sad that he made a really bad choice to walk away from his family but he is the one who has to answer to the Lord. Yes, his bad choices did affect my life but that does not mean I can hold unforgiveness in my heart against him. I can truly say I have forgiven my dad for all that happened when I was a child. I love him because he is my dad. I do not always agree with him but I do not hold things against him anymore.

We have to be careful to guard our hearts continually even in places that have been healed. If we do not, the Enemy can slip in and begin to steal the things the Lord has done. It could happen by someone's words about that person or just a negative thought he brings to us. If we dwell on those thoughts, they can become roots that will try to destroy all the Lord has done for us.

I am grateful the Lord healed our relationship and that I do know my dad. He is not perfect, and I still get mad at him sometimes but he has become my hero as he was always supposed to be. I am thankful the Lord encouraged me to open my heart and allow my dad back in there. We have talked about all the regrets he has about that time in his life. I know he has to deal with those things with the Lord. It's probably been ten years or more now since he came to the Lord. I am thankful he has gotten saved and that I have the promise of seeing him in heaven someday.

The little girl who always wanted her daddy right there beside her can truly say the Lord has done a marvelous work. That which the Enemy meant for bad, God turned around and made it better. I am so thankful. I love my dad, and I know he loves me; that is truly all that really matters.

Now, when I go to my heart's garden where I keep my thoughts about my dad, all I see are beautiful roses of every color. No more locked gates and brick walls standing there. No more frozen memories! The keys to that part of my heart will forever be in God's hands. The ruins have been restored and there is nothing but peace and freedom in that area now.

Chapter 7

THE RUINS - MY MOM

After my heart was healed in relation to my dad, I knew there would be more walls to tear down. I wanted change and I sought it. My Prince never forced me to move forward. He knew I would have to be willing to go there. It was like I could walk in peace for a while and then I was restless for change. I would start crying out to the Lord, "Please change me!" He was always faithful to show me the way. The more time I spent with Him, the more I wanted to be healed in all areas.

I was again led to the Grace course and the next area the Lord worked on was my relationship with my mom. That was a very hard area for me because I had such abandonment and rejection issues. I wanted her approval so much all my life. I was angry inside at her but I could never let her know because I feared her rejection and anger. I feared her even into adulthood. I never stood up to her until the Lord told me to. For all those years, I lived in fear of her because I wanted her approval. As a result, I let her treat me however she chose to. I always felt because she was my mom, she had a right to verbally abuse me.

As a child, I could not do anything right to please my mom. Not that she meant to make me feel unwanted but that is how I always felt. As mentioned before, I always thought she never wanted me or loved me. From birth, till age nine, I was tossed back and forth between my grandparents and her. Most of the time was spent in my grandparents care. At times, I thought my mom didn't really care if she had me with her or not. You know, as a child, you can only see the things that hurt you. The Enemy will build on those things to deceive you. He uses those things to make you believe you are not wanted.

My grandpa became my hero because he was always there for me when I needed him. He always stepped in to protect me from my mom when she wanted to beat me with that belt. I am sure, at times, I probably needed it but most of the time it was my older brother blaming me for things I did not do. He was always my mom's favorite so he did no wrong in her eyes.

I have vivid memories of her driving into the driveway and my brother running to tell her all I had done that day. Then she would scream my name and say she was going to beat me with that belt. I would usually run and hide in the closet hoping she would not find me. Most of my childhood, I felt like an outcast, awkward, and unloved. Kind of like the Ugly Duckling!

When my mom decided to move to California, I believe my grandpa pressured her to leave me with him. I do not think she wanted to leave me but she really had no choice because there was no room in the U-Haul truck that was carrying all my aunt's things. My two brothers were barely able to fit in there. I will never forget the day my mom told me I had to stay at my grandparents' house. She asked me to go for a ride around the block in the big U-Haul truck. As I climbed up in it, I thought I was in trouble again.

My mom started telling me I would have to stay with my grandparents because she did not have room for me in the truck. I started to cry, and she told me it would only be for a year. She said she could not afford to take me and that it would be better for me to stay. She then told me if I would stay that I could have the silver locket with pictures of my dad and her and her Disney bracelet. I agreed to it because I had no other choice.

I had already been through so much where we lived with all my cousins. I was teased and told I was fat and ugly all the time by all of them. I was told to disappear and never be seen. When we sat down to eat dinner, I was laughed at and called fat if I ate more than what they thought I should. All my girl cousins around my age were little and thin, and I was not built that way. I was ridiculed all the time. My aunt never corrected her children when they insulted me. It was probably permitted because they thought it would help me in some way. So when my mom drove me around that block and told me that, I was a little relieved inside. At least, I would not have to be ridiculed any longer by that family.

When we drove back into that drive way, there stood my grandpa. I jumped out of that truck and ran into his loving arms. He embraced me, and I told him, "I am going to get to live with you Grandpa." I remember him saying, "Yes, I know; now, go and play."

I remember my mom and I sleeping in that big four poster bed and her wrapping me up in her arms and telling me how much she loved me and was going to miss me. I think I heard her but so much had happened that I was just glad I was going to stay with my grandparents for a while. I was tired of moving all the time. I just wanted to live in one place, finally. The next morning when she left, I stood on that porch with my grandparents after she had hugged and kissed me waving goodbye. Little did I know I would never live with my mom and brothers again.

I remember that first night there, my grandpa and grandma tucked me in and told me how much they loved me. My grandpa told me I was home now and I was to have sweet dreams. I snuggled deep under those covers that my grandma had washed and hung on the clothes line to dry that day. I smelled the sunshine and fell off to sleep knowing I was safe.

I had felt so unloved and unwanted by both my parents and now I really felt like I had totally lost my family. I would miss my brothers so much in the years to come. My big brothers were not there to protect me from those who would tease and torment me as I grew up. I missed just being able to spend time with them.

My grandparents did their best for me. They were not well off so to take me in put a strain on them. My grandma had to get a job after a while so they could support me.

It took a long time to let the Lord deal with this part of my heart. I tried many times on my own to surrender it all to Him but I would lay it down and then pick it up again until I finally realized He loved me and just wanted me to be well. I realized also that I did not need anyone's approval but His. Healing became easier at that point. However, with my mom, it took longer for me to see all the Lord needed me to see.

I had spent more time with my mom than with my dad. I think that's why the Enemy had spent more time feeding me lies about my mom not wanting or loving me.

When I stepped into that area of my heart with my Jesus, which had all those bad memories locked up about my mom, all I saw were weeds and thorns. I also saw this huge vine that wrapped itself around all the trees and everything growing there. It was a very thick and deep-rooted vine. I looked at my Prince and fell on my knees, asking Him to forgive me for allowing this to consume my heart's garden. He took me by the hand and said, "All is washed away my daughter." I then stood and asked Him what this deep-rooted vine was about. Then He showed me how the Enemy had planted a lie in my heart when I was little. That lie had become so much a part of my belief that it consumed me. He said the more I believed that lie, the more that vine grew. The lie was that my mom did not love or want me when she really did.

As I began to look back, I could see how I looked at things through my childish eyes. At that point, the Lord opened them to see the truth. I always thought she did not love me because it seemed she never had time for me. I was always with my grandparents and at night, they tucked me in, not her. Her boyfriends consumed her time. I did not realize that she was still a young woman when I was little and that she too was looking for acceptance.

Then the Lord showed me how my mom had so many regrets in her life. She regretted all the bad choices she had made. One of them was that she felt she was a failure as a mom to me. She also felt such remorse over having to leave me with my grandparents. When she came back a year later to get me, I refused to go with her. My grandpa had filled my head with so much stuff that I was afraid to go with her then. I think he was afraid of never seeing me again also. That vine that had woven its way throughout my heart and life was now finally being cut down by my Prince of Peace. It no longer could hold me captive. It was thrown into the fire never to be seen again.

I will always love my mom; however, I finally had to realize it was not about her accepting me anymore. Rather, it was that she operated out of a place of hurt herself and all that matters is she loved me. The only one I ever needed to accept me is my Jesus. I took care of my mom for a year when

I was around fifty and at first, it was good but then she got restless as she always would do. She wanted to move back with my niece twelve hours from me. It was really hard to let her go because all her family was here but I had to because she insisted that she was not happy.

We did not talk for a long while. Finally, the Lord told me I needed to forgive her and let all that go. It was around that time the Lord started healing my heart. He told me that it was time for my mom to know that I forgave her. By this time, she was in a nursing home. I would call her every so often and talk with her. She would always remember me and was happy to hear from me.

The Lord allowed me to visit her twice before she passed away. I remember the first time very well. I walked into the dining room where she was eating breakfast. I went up beside her and gave her a hug and said, "What you doing Momma?" She looked at me and said, "Just where have you been?"

I laughed and said, "Back home in Missouri."

She said, "Oh that's far away."

She told the nurses that I was her baby girl. That brought tears to my eyes. We took a couple of pictures, and I will treasure them forever.

I could only stay a couple of days but I was so thankful for the time I spent there with her. While I was there, I bought her a baby doll. She carried that baby doll with her everywhere. She named it Victoria. When I went back the second time, she was holding her baby doll and talking to her; it was so sweet. She loved that baby doll till the day she passed away.

As I sat and cried over losing her, I began to pray and thank the Lord that He had healed our relationship. I also thanked Him for saving her and rescuing her from all her sorrows. I thanked Him that I would one day see her again. At that time, I asked Him to give me some good memories about my momma that I could hold in my heart.

I knew already that she had loved me when I was a child. He showed me how it broke her heart when she had to leave me with my grandparents. He told me that when she came back to get me and I would not go with her, she closed her heart off. She was broken and lost at that point. Her greatest fear had come true. She had lost her baby girl and did not know how to get me back.

He then reminded me of all the good my momma had given me when I was young. Even though she only had those first nine years, she gave me so many good memories of how much she really did love me.

Yes, she was hard on me but I was spoiled rotten by my grandpa. I was always doing something that I probably should not have been doing. My brothers were always helping me get into trouble too. Like the time she left us in the car while she went into the store. It was around Christmas and someone had given her a box of Russell Stover's chocolates. We got bored in the car waiting so we got into the candy and ate every piece of it. Or the time we opened all our Christmas presents before Christmas.

My brother next to me was only two years older, and we were always doing something. One time, we took our Dr. Seuss books and cut all the pictures out of them. Many times, we would jump on my mom's bed doing summersaults. We knew we were not supposed to but we did it anyway. My mom had her hands full with three small children. Even though she was hard on us, I can now see why. We were stinkers!

She may have been hard at times but then there were the times she would tell us she loved us every day. "A bushel and a peck and a hug around our neck." I remember the tickles and hugs and so much laughter we had with each other before my stepfather came into the picture. She would hug me at night when she was there and tell me she loved me. On the weekends, she would always try and do things with us like going to the drive-in, to the lake in the summer camping, to the zoo or on a picnic in the park. Her favorite was going to Dairy Queen and getting an ice cream cone. We had a mom who really did love us even though she had problems.

I believe most of my family thought I did not love my momma but they were so wrong. I loved her very much. She is the reason why family has always been so important to me, the reason why I love my children and grandchildren dearly. It is sad that the Enemy stole so much from my momma and me but in the end, God gave it all back to me. She was saved in 2004, so I have the assurance I will see her again. She is finally at peace with the Lord. So in the end we both win!

Today, I have great peace in my heart in relation to my mom. I have a beautiful place of peace and rest with pretty purple roses growing everywhere. A place that has been rebuilt with such love and care by my Prince of Peace.

Chapter 8

THE RUINS -MY STEPFATHER

How do I begin to tell you about a man who hurt me so cruelly as a little girl? He walked into my life when I was about four. He was another one of my mom's men whom she had met at a bar or through a friend. He won me over by being nice and acting like he cared.

It's kind of interesting how men like him become part of your family. It seems like they set their eyes upon their goals and then go after conquering them through their kindness until they have their prizes before them. Then after they have won, they no longer have to be so kind. They become totally different people. Then your family is torn and driven by the pain they inflict on everyone.

My mom married him when I was five years old, and we moved into a house around the corner from my grandparents. He had three sons who moved in with us too. So we went from a family of four to a family of eight. I was the youngest and the only girl. I imagine my mom thought it would be perfect with his children and her children all becoming a family. Actually, everyone thought it was a loving home; however, that was so far from the truth. It became a home of fear and trepidation — anything but love.

At first, my stepfather was the same as he had always been until we moved in. He decided that because we did not have a father in our lives he would be our father. He wormed his way into my little girl's heart of trust by being a so-called father figure to me. I did not really know what a father was supposed to be like since my daddy was not around. I assumed this was how it was supposed to be.

120

I was a busy child and was spoiled by my grandpa who hardly ever spanked me. Now, every time I even did any small thing wrong, I was yelled at, beaten with a belt or had to go pick my switch off the weeping willow tree. I remember he was always holding me on his lap and one day he touched me. I tried to get away but he held me so I could not. He told me that the more I fought him the more tightly he was going to squeeze me, and he did. When I told him I was going to tell my grandpa, he told me if I told anyone, he would take the shotguns in my grandpa's cabinet and kill my whole family. Fear settled in my heart at that moment and continued growing in me until years and years later when God finally got into my dungeon and healed that deep wound.

By the time I started school, he had been molesting me for over a year. He continued to beat me with his belt and it seemed to get worse every time. I became a very shy, withdrawn child and was so full of fear that I would barely talk to an adult. I had a hard time learning to read or anything. I believe all of that had to do with all I was going through at home.

In those days, teachers seldom asked questions about your home life. I do not know if they did not care but maybe it was because back then kids had no say about anything. You did what you were told and if you did not, you were beaten with a belt. It taught us respect for sure but it also taught us to never speak up for ourselves against an adult. Many people my age suffered some terrible wrongs when they were young just like I did.

In those days, I was dropped off at my grandparent's house every morning as my mom and stepfather headed off to work. I would then get on the bus and ride to school. As said earlier, for the most part, I hated school because I felt so ugly and unwanted there. I was always teased by the other children. I was always fat, ugly and stupid. They would not let me in Brownies like my cousins because my mom did not have the money. It was always something so I became a "nothing" for the most part. I tried to be good but in order to get attention in class I acted badly. I think I figured because I could not do anything good enough for anyone, I would just be a bad girl.

When I came home from school, I would again be at my grandparent's house waiting for my mom and stepfather to get home. Usually, I would play with my brothers and my cousins. I was always teased by them as well it seemed. My cousin Sandy and my brother Michael next to me seemed to be the only ones who really liked me; however, sometimes, they would not even play with me.

After a while, my stepfather would always show up first to pick me up. Usually, my brothers would be out with their friends playing in the neighborhood. We did not live far from my grandparents, so they could walk home when it was time to come in for dinner.

Those were days when children played outside until the street lights came on. However, I had to be picked up by my stepfather. We would head home to that house and because no one was home, it was his perfect opportunity to take advantage of me. He would always start out by making me take a bath touching me and making me touch him. If I cooperated with him, I was not beaten that day and if I did not cooperate then he would pull out his belt and beat me with it. I was then sent to my room or downstairs out of his sight.

He would always tell me I was worthless and no one wanted me. This became such a regular occurrence that I believed him. He told me my mom really did not love me and never wanted me and that my dad never wanted me either. I was convinced I was not loved.

As the molesting continued day after day, I began to go to what I call my dream world to escape all the pain I felt in my heart. I felt like I had no one to talk to so I dreamed of a better place and there, I first began to see my Jesus. When all the abuse that I faced on a daily basis became too much for me I would run into my room and close my door. I would lie on my bed and cry. In those moments, I would hear a quiet voice saying, "Tammy, come and sit with Me awhile." So I would allow myself to go into this world where I felt so safe.

I would be standing in this field of flowers so tall with every color that you can imagine. I would twirl around and around until I would fall to the ground. Then I would lay there looking up at the sky and watch the clouds floating by. I would soak in all that beauty that was surrounding me, because I knew it would not be long until I had to leave that beautiful place.

As I lay there dreaming away in that garden I would hear footsteps coming through those flowers, and I would stand up to see my Jesus coming to see me. I would always rush into His wide open arms. He would pick me up and twirl me around as I held Him so tight. Then He would kiss me on my cheek and tell me He loved me as we laughed. He would sit me down and we would walk through those tall flowers as we talked about so many things.

I could tell Him everything. I never worried when I was with Him in those moments' I always knew I was safe beside Him. There was a tree in that garden that was down by a stream. On that big tree was a swing and we would go sit on that swing together and talk about all my fears and things that had hurt me that day. He would always tell me it would be okay and that He was always with me. I so much wanted to stay in that place where I felt safe but I knew it would end at some point, and I would have to go back to the real world. There were so many days spent in that garden with my Jesus that the real world and my place of dreams seemed to collide.

I was caught in this evil house with these evil things happening to me. As the beatings increased, my mom tried to step in to protect me but my stepfather wanted nothing to do with that. I did not realize until years later that he was beating her as well. I remember the verbal abuse that she suffered at his hands because we all had that but because I blocked most of that terrible time in my life, I did not remember the beatings she received until the Lord brought it to my remembrance years later.

After so long, I think I just became so numb to the molesting and the beatings that I figured this was the way it would always be for worthless and unwanted me. I think he must have gotten tired of just doing what he was doing because then he started doing a little more, and I started fighting with him. The beatings became worse every time I fought with him. Some days, he would beat me until my legs bled.

On those days, I would run into the basement, shut the door and go curl up in the corner to hide from him and the world. I hoped he would never find me again. I would cry and cry for hours; my lips would quiver in such great fear that he would come again to get me. I truly did not even understand what he was doing to me or even why he was doing it. I was too young to even grasp the meaning of sex at that time of my life, nor did I want to. All I knew is this man who was supposed to love and protect me was abusing me in such a way that as a little girl I could not even comprehend. When he was molesting me every day, he was telling me that he loved me and that is what daddy's do to their little girls. But even in my little understanding, I knew somehow it was wrong and not true because why would a daddy want to hurt his little girl so badly.

I thought that I just had to keep letting him do to me what he wanted or he would kill my family. In my mind, I did not understand how if it was right, why I couldn't tell anyone or he would hurt my family. I finally justified in myself that it had to be a very bad secret that I was keeping from everyone. I had always been a story teller, so I knew no one would ever believe me. I was the little girl no one wanted and who felt so unloved. I lived in my dream world most of the time just so I could survive the pain in my heart.

In those days a child was to be seen and never heard; so for me to accuse a man of these things, I would have to tell the right person. I hung on as long as I could until the day that he raped me. I was about to turn seven, and he said it was my birthday present. He said I was old enough now to do more for him. I remember he picked me up as usual from my grandparent's house and drove me home. By then, it was summer time and school was out. I had spent the day with my grandparents playing outside with my cousins. I was hot and sweaty when he picked me up that day.

When we got home he told me to get undressed and get in the bath tub. I did as he said, and he came in as usual to wash me and touch me. This time, however, he got in the tub with me and began to force himself on me. I fought him as much as I could but he put his hand on my throat and began to choke me. He said if I fought him then I was going to be sorry. I tried not to struggle but it was hard. He forced himself all the way in my little body that day and I screamed in pain. He dunked my head under the water and said if I screamed again he would drown me. I cried and cried but I did not scream.

When he was done, he got up off me and got out of the tub. He pulled me up with blood running down my legs. He put me in a towel, took me in my room and beat me with his belt for screaming and crying. Then he told me to get dressed and get out of his sight. He told me that next time I better not scream or it would be the last time I did.

I dressed myself as I continued to cry and as the blood ran down my legs, not only from what he had done to me but from the beating. I ran as fast as I could downstairs to that dark corner in the basement and tried to hide. I rolled up in a ball as tight as I could because I was in so much pain and I was so afraid he was coming to get me again. I was down there a long time that day.

My mom came and called me to dinner. When she saw me, she told me to go to my room and clean myself up. My stepfather told her I had been bad that day and that I deserved a spanking because I would not listen to him. She did not argue with him because she believed him.

I was sent to bed that night without dinner and my mom told me I know when I did not obey him I was going to be beaten. She said, "You need to try harder to obey him Tammy." I never told my Mom the truth of that day until I was in my thirties. When I told her, she was shocked I had gone through what I did. She told me she never knew it happened and she was so sorry it did. She said that my grandpa never told her anything.

While I was down in that basement I went into my dream world with all my tears. I ran to my Jesus and told him everything. I asked Him why this man kept hurting me. He told me I needed to tell on him before he hurt me again. I was so afraid to tell but He told me I needed to, and He would give me courage to tell. I asked Jesus who I should tell because I thought I could trust no one to believe me. He told me to tell my grandpa. I decided that He was right and somehow, in those moments of sitting with Jesus, He gave me enough courage to tell my grandpa all the bad things my stepfather had done to me. I cried when I left my dream place that day because I did not want to go back to that pain anymore. Jesus gave me courage to hold on to Him.

The next day as I went to my grandparents' house, I hung close to my grandpa all day. I was his shadow most of the time anyway. I knew I would have to stay close by him and wait for the perfect opportunity to spill all this out to him. He told me several times to go play with my cousins but I kept saying, "Grandpa, can I just stay with you today?" He never asked why but just kept letting me follow him around. Grandma asked him to go to the store later that day, and I knew I had to go with him if I was going to ever tell him. I begged him to let me go with him and, of course, he said yes.

As we drove up to the corner market I was really quiet. Grandpa asked me several times what was wrong and why I was so quiet. I did not answer him until he stopped the car at the market. I began by asking him if it was wrong to keep a secret. He then told me that secrets are okay to keep if they are good ones, like if you know what someone is getting for her birthday or maybe a Christmas present. Then he said, "However if someone is stealing or doing a bad thing, it is wrong to keep it a secret."

I started to cry, and I told him that I had a really bad secret to tell him. He reached over and pulled me close to him and put his arm around me. He took my chin and lifted it up and said, "Pussycat (my nickname he always called me), you know you can tell your grandpa anything."

So I spilled everything out to him. I left nothing out. I told him all the details of that horrible time and that I was afraid. He reassured me that it was going to be okay now and that my stepfather would never hurt me again. He never went into the market that day. He turned the car around and went straight home. He told me to go play with my cousins and not be afraid. He took my grandma in the other room and told her what had happened.

When my stepfather came to the door that night to pick me up, he walked in as usual and said, "Come on." My grandpa stepped in front of him and told him that he would never touch me again, and I was not going anywhere with him." They got into a terrible argument and they started fighting as he tried to grab me. He broke my grandpa's glasses and my grandpa threw him out of the house.

He told him he had better get his stuff out of that house and be gone. He yelled at me several times that he was going to come back and get me for telling. As he finally left, I ran out from under the table and into my grandma's arms crying. My grandpa got his shotgun out and loaded it. He went down to that house and escorted him out of there.

Although we never saw him again, he did follow us around many times. He broke into our home and got all his things out. My mom soon sold that house, and we moved back in with my grandparents. I am not sure what my grandpa actually told my mom as to why my stepdad left but she always said she never knew what he had done to me. She said that my grandpa never told her anything that had happened.

My grandparent's never asked me about what happened anymore, and I never wanted to talk about it. It became this big, dark secret that was deeply buried in my heart where I thought no one would ever find it again.

Many times after I was saved, I went to the Lord and asked Him to forgive me, and I tried very hard to forgive this man who had hurt me so badly. I actually thought I had forgiven him especially after the first time the prophet spoke into my life and told me about being in the corner of the basement. After that, I thought it was all over, and I would get better. But that was only the beginning of the healing process. I had to go through many more steps in the process of healing before this area was fully addressed and healed. I believe because it was so rooted inside me that it had to be taken out step by step. I still believe, as I have said already, that if the Lord had done a deep healing right away, I am not sure I would have been able to handle it.

There I was, a grown woman stuck in the emotional entrapment of a seven-year- old. It was almost like God was taking me back one step and one person at a time for some reason. I found out the reason in 2006 when I was helping with a ministry. I had already been through the Grace course several times and had been asked to be a leader in the next session. I agreed to do it and during that time, I realized I still needed healing in my life. I pulled another leader aside and asked if I could have a time of prayer with them. When asked why, I explained that in my heart, I felt there was something deep that needed to come forth. I said, "I do not know what it is; however, I feel in my spirit that it is urgent and needs to be dealt with." The leader agreed to set aside a time to minister to me. I had been there before with the same two women ministering to me so I was comfortable with them.

We started out just talking, and they asked me about family members and if I had forgiven them. They asked about my stepfather and immediately, I became that little girl so afraid. I was rocking back and forth and began to scream out: "He is coming; he is coming to get me!" My lips trembled and I shook very hard as I cried with overwhelming fear. I really scared my friends who were in that ministry time with me.

However, Debbie began to pray as did the other lady. Debbie got down on her knees in front of me and grabbed my hands as I continued to scream, "He is coming. He is coming!" She said, "Tammy, Tammy, Tammy" loudly. She could not get me to calm down. It was like this overwhelming fear had gripped every part of my being. She said, "God did not give you a spirit of fear but of a sound mind," repeatedly, until the Holy Spirit took over and calmed me down. All fear was broken from me that day. All fear of man and the unknown. I was finally free of that dungeon I had been avoiding for years.

Thank God for those women of God who were prayed up and ready to take on the Enemy because if they were not there, the Enemy might have kept me in that state of fear. Thank God He chose not to leave me in that mindset but to set me free.

Fear is an awful thing when it is so deep inside you. I did not even realize that fear was the root of all my fears in life. It is why I could not go forward in the Lord because I did not really know how to trust Him. I allowed everyone to rule my life out of fear for them because it ruled my heart. When I left there that day, I felt like a ton of bricks had been lifted off my shoulders. I went home and lay on my bed, resting and thanking the Lord for delivering me from the bondage of fear.

As I began to pray, the Lord asked me if I would like to see what happened when I went to that place. I said, "Yes Lord, as long as You go there with me." He said, "Take my hand and we will go." I closed my eyes and as soon as I did, the Lord was standing beside me. We were at the steps that led down to that dungeon. As He urged me on, I stepped down, and He was behind me. Then all of a sudden, I saw myself in the corner of that basement curled up in the corner. I was that little girl again, sobbing so deeply and crying. "He is going to get me." Then I heard footsteps coming down those stairs. I shook with great fear and my lips quivered as I cried even more. As I heard the door open, I hid my face in my hands and curled up. The person was coming closer over to me but I was so afraid to look up and see who it was because of all that fear.

The man squatted down to my level right in front of me but still, I cried and I would not look. Then He stretched His hand to me, gently, lifted my head,- and looked me in the eyes. I looked at Him and realized it was my Prince kneeling before me. He took my hands in His and said, "Baby girl, are you ready to get out of this place now?" I nodded yes. He picked me up and carried me up those steps out of that place of fear forevermore. That is where I am today and will be forever in His loving arms. I no longer have to fear anything because He has conquered all my fears.

I do not have to fear that place anymore because I know who has me in His arms, my Prince of Peace. He rules and reigns totally in my heart today. That dungeon area of fear has been washed clean now. It is a beautiful sunroom full of peace and joy.

God never leaves us undone; He always finishes what He starts even if it takes years to complete. He peels back layer after layer to finish His work in us. We have to be willing to accept that peeling process though. He leaves nothing missing and nothing broken. They say time heals all wounds, but I say God is the only one who can take a broken little girl so full of fear, doubt, and unbelief and heal her completely.

I was no longer that little girl in a grown woman's body. I truly found my way that day to walk forward and learn how to trust the Lord with all my heart and everything that is within me. I could finally waltz through that part of my heart's garden and have peace. I no longer had to fear Jesus wanting to go there. I gave Him my all that day forever.

I am so very thankful for all He has done for me. In my quiet times, I close my eyes and see Him waiting there for me. As I walk into the throne room, He puts His scepter forth for me to come. He steps down from His throne, comes to me and kisses me on the cheek. He takes my hand, and as beautiful music plays He says, "Come, dance with Me, My love," and we waltz around that beautiful place that is filled with His mercy and grace. My heart fills with great joy just knowing that all I have to do is close my eyes, say His name and I am there.

Chapter 9

THE RUINS - MY DAUGHTER'S FATHER

As a young girl, I grew up really sheltered by my grandpa and grandma. I believe after I had finally told my grandpa what my stepfather had done to me that he became even more protective. I was not even allowed out of my yard or to play with the neighborhood kids after my mom and brothers left. I got my first bike when I was twelve and loved riding it but I was only allowed to the second driveway from my home. At school, I was not a popular girl at all. I had only a few close friends. When I turned fourteen, I met a new friend in school. She talked me into a lot of things that I probably never would have done on my own. One of those was to rebel against my grandparents.

I started going to her church on a bus, and I would usually go home with her afterwards. I spent a lot of weekends over at her house. She did not like being at my house because we had a curfew. This went on for a couple years during junior high school. Then we went to high school. We were separated by school boundaries. We went to rival schools at that point. However, we still saw each other at church and the weekends.

She was a popular girl and had a boyfriend right away but her parents did not approve of him. However, they did approve of his best friend. So in order for her to date her boyfriend, she had to tell many lies. She decided to set me up with his friend. In late October, she had a party, and he came by for a few minutes. It was there I was introduced to Jim. Then in December at a friend's party, he was also there. I remember when I walked in he was lying on the floor with a girl making out. I should have turned around and ran then but I did not. I sat there as the usual outcast until finally, I left with another group of friends.

Then on New Year's Eve, my friend talked me into going to another party with her. We had been at a church function but we decided to go party somewhere else. We ended up where he was. He had been drinking and was pretty toasted by the time I came around. His other friend decided he liked me and started talking to me. He was pretty toasted himself and really just wanted to make out with someone. At that point in my life, I thought I was so worthless. I felt ugly, fat, and very unwanted. I had never had a date, and I had never been kissed or even held a boy's hand. I thought because I was sixteen and ugly that no one would ever love me. I assumed that if a guy was acting like he liked me, it was a good thing.

This guy wanted to take me home but Jim stepped in and said, "No, I will take you both home because I have to take my other friends home." That guy was all over me in the backseat, and Jim kept watching in the rearview mirror. When Jim got to the guy's house he told him to get out. Then he told me that I needed to leave that guy alone because he was bad news. My friend was up in the front seat all over Jim because she really liked both him and her boyfriend. She would lie to her parents and tell them that she was going out with Jim.

She finally set Jim and me up on a date and, of course, she and her boyfriend went along. We did not really talk much; we just made out in a parked car. Again because of my low self-image, I assumed that the only way to get love was by kissing and allowing him to touch me. I knew in my heart it was wrong but inside I just really wanted someone to love me. We talked all the time on the phone, and he let me wear his class ring. I really thought I was big stuff because finally, I was feeling loved by someone.

I remember meeting his parents for the first time. They seemed nice. I liked his dad but I could tell his mom really did not care for me at all. We were all downstairs playing pool, and we were laughing having a good time. His mom happened to walk in when he kissed me and pulled me on his lap. She told him she was not going to have that kind of stuff going on. My friend told me later that his mom thought I was from the bad side of town because I came from a poor family.

Jim and I continued to date and on Valentine's Day, he cooked me a beautiful dinner and gave me flowers. That night, he told me he loved me. I remember saying, "No you don't" but he said, "Yes, I really do." I was head over heels in love with him. At that point, I would have done anything to make him happy. I was still attending church but I would ride the bus there and then leave and go down the street to meet him. He really wanted nothing to do with church. A few weeks later after my choir concert, we went out parking in his car. We went all the way that night in the midst of all the passion.

For some reason, I seemed to know at that moment that I was pregnant. I remember going to McDonald's afterward, and I went in the bathroom to cry. I was so scared but I pretended I wasn't. He was as comforting as he could be during the next few weeks. When I missed my period, I knew for sure I was pregnant. I started getting sick at that point. My grandma suspected something because I was so sick every day.

My friend finally told her mom, and she took me to a doctor to be checked. I remember them telling me I was pregnant, and I stood there crying. I walked up to his school to meet him that day to let him know in person. When he saw me, he was cold as ice and called me by my last name. I told him and he said he already knew; my friend had told him. I asked him what we were going to do and all he could say was, "I don't know. Let me figure it out. Do not tell my family."

After a couple of days, I told my grandparents because I could not go on lying to them. Then my grandma told my aunt and her kids. They all wanted me to abort the baby because I was too young to keep her, and I couldn't provide for her. I kept saying, "Jim and I are keeping our baby" but they were insistent that I abort her. Jim would not tell his parents. A week later, my aunt called his mom and told her. She then called a big meeting at their house to discuss what was going to be done.

The day I walked into that house with my aunt beside me, it was like going into a war zone. The enemy, his mother mainly, had already decided what was going to be done. All she needed to do now was tell me what I had to do. I was told I was not going to keep my baby; that we were too young, and Jim had plans for his life. The most important thing was for him to finish high school. He had two months left, and I had two years.

Oh, he sat beside me holding my hand and trying to be the man but I think he knew at that point he had better agree with his mom or else. It seemed like she lectured us forever because I kept saying, "I want to keep my baby." Then she told us to go in his room and talk about what we were going to do.

I do not remember everything that we said to each other that night but we finally agreed it was best to abort our baby. At one point he said, "There are baby clothes in the attic." He laughed and said, "But it's crazy to believe we could raise a child." I loved him so much that I would have done whatever he said at that point. I was so afraid to speak up for myself because I just wanted him to love me and our child. We went out there to that war room and told his family we were going to abort the baby. His mom said, "Well, he will be beside you when it's done, like that was supposed to solve something." I was told to find a place to have it done and let them know.

That next week, I cried and cried because I already loved my baby. I wanted to keep her no matter if he did or not. I called several places but always put it on hold. Finally, one day, his mom called and said, "Have you set a date and time to have this done yet?" I hesitated and said, "I am not sure if I want to do it or not." She became so angry at me. I went home that night and as I lay on my bed crying, I asked the Lord to forgive me for all I had done. I made a promise to Him that if He would let me keep my baby, I would serve Him. I went to my grandpa the next day and told him that I really wanted to keep my baby. He told my grandma that he had a dream the night before in which the Lord told him to let me keep the baby. I thanked him and thanked the Lord. I knew I was going to have to face Jim and his parents soon.

The next day, I went back into his parents' war zone but I did so knowing my grandparents and the Lord were on my side. I told them I was keeping my baby no matter what they said or what Jim did. His mother was furious and said I had no business keeping my baby. Jim and I went into his room again and talked. This time, he was very angry at me. He told me I was just doing this to get back at my grandpa and some other awful things. He threw my class ring at me and told me he never wanted to see my face again. I got up and walked out of that house without ever saying goodbye.

Three days later, I was at my friend's house, and we walked up to our hangout to eat. Jim showed up, wrapped his arms around me, and kissed me. I pushed his hands down, turned around, looked him in the eyes, and said, "You said you never wanted to see me again." He said, "That was the other day, not now." I was still so hurt inside that I pushed him away.

Our friend got married a couple months later, and I was her maid of honor. Jim was there, and he was so angry he would not even talk to me. We never spoke again until after our daughter was born.

The church I was attending at the time rejected me and the youth pastor came to my house but would not come in. He told me to abort my baby or give it up for adoption. If I chose not to do either of them, I would never be welcomed at their church again. By then, I was strong enough to stand up for what I wanted so I told him I was keeping my baby, and I would never return to their church.

I did not tell any of my family that I was pregnant. My grandparents thought it best not to say anything. My one aunt who lived there was the only one who knew. I decided to go back to school but after attending the first few days and being laughed at and judged, I decided it was probably best not to. However, I ended up getting my GED.

My grandpa got really sick in October of that year and had to be placed in a nursing home. He became very violent with my grandma at times. He was at the beginning stages of Alzheimer's disease. Because of that, I had to finally tell my family that I was pregnant. Mom was furious, of course, and wanted me to abort. By then, I was far enough along that it was not going to happen.

My grandma was so good to me and stood by me as my aunts and uncles put their opinions in. Grandma helped me fix up a small nursery for my daughter and made her some special things. My mom and brothers came back for Thanksgiving that year because my baby was due right around then. My brother Michael stayed to help drive me to the hospital.

One day, my uncle came to our house with his little folder in his hands and sat my grandma down to tell her what I was going to do with my child. He told her I was going to have to give my baby up for adoption. He had it all laid out in a plan for her to see. She listened and then she said to him, "This is my house; she will stay here, and she will keep her child because that is what is best for her and that is what your dad and I agreed to do." Basically, she told him to get out of her business. My grandma also reminded him he had three daughters not raised yet and asked if that had ever happened to one of them if he would make her give up the baby? My uncle never interfered after that.

When my daughter was born a couple of weeks later, I was living in so much fear that someone was going to steal her. I had no peace. I came close to losing my life during my delivery because I hemorrhaged. I would not let my grandma call Jim to let him know I was having our daughter. As my grandma and brother waited for me outside the delivery room, they could hear me crying. My grandma was so worried about me and the baby. I would find out years later that she had lost her firstborn child.

When my daughter was born, I heard her cry and my heart was so overjoyed. They cleaned her up, and I could only look at her because back then, they did not let you hold the baby right away. After about two hours of them trying to get the bleeding under control, the doctor knew my family would be worried, so he sent the nurse out to tell my grandma I was okay. They wanted me to be able to tell them if I had a girl or boy.

My daughter continued to cry so they wrapped her up in the warmer and took her down to the nursery. My family finally saw her but did not know if my baby was a girl or boy. The doctor continued working on me for another hour. So to ease my family's worries about me, they wrapped my daughter in blue and all the other babies in pink. That day, she was the only girl in the nursery. They were finally allowed to see her.

When I got to my room, my grandma and brother came in and congratulated me. My brother said, "Well, too bad you got a boy," and my grandma said, "Oh, well, we will love him." I said, "What, I did not have a boy; I had a little girl." My brother was insistent that I had a boy, and I was insistent I had a girl. So he went back down to the nursery; they had switched her into pink and all the boys back to blue. My grandma and brother were so happy that I had a girl! When they finally brought her to me, she was still crying. They put her in my arms and she stopped crying and just looked at me. My heart had already fallen in love with her but now, I could see my beautiful baby I had waited so long to hold.

I had to stay in the hospital longer so I could be given blood transfusions. I finally told my grandma to call my two friends. I did not have her call Jim because I still feared his parents would take my daughter away from me. He found out through our friend. She went to his house gloating about it and passing out cigars to him. It made him even angrier that I did not call him myself. He did not come to see me. My family continued to be angry that I had kept my baby but I did not care. I knew it was the right thing for me to do.

Jim and I saw each other about a month later and he saw our daughter for the first time. He really did not have much to say. He held her for a few minutes and then handed her back to me. We talked a few times but he really wanted nothing to do with me. He was heading to the service and did not want anyone hanging on his back. I saw him again when our daughter was six months old. We talked again but he really was too busy playing the field to be bothered with me or our daughter. He basically told me that he never wanted to see my face again. That broke my heart but I went on.

At that point, I thought no one would ever love me. Now, not only was I a single mom but I felt even more unloved and unwanted. About a year later, I heard he had gotten married. His mom found someone she approved of from the right side of town. All my hopes and dreams of him ever coming back vanished at that point. I felt very alone but I knew I had to keep on going because my daughter needed me. I dealt with great depression because of all the issues in my past. My daughter became the reason why I got up in the mornings. Someone needed me.

I started dating my husband a few months after that happened. Of course, I went down a road of not walking with God and running after the world. I was so confused inside. I thought you had to give a man everything in order for him to love you. I had that all wrong inside.

I buried all the hurt and pain of Jim so deep in my heart that it even hurt to go there. I did write Jim several times over the years. I knew where he was for the most part. I would send the letters to his parents and they would pass them on to him. He never responded. As my daughter got older, she wanted to know him. I always told her the truth because I believed God wanted it that way. I also did it because I knew I would always love her father, and I wanted him to know her. She was not a mistake like he had been told. She was a gift from God!

When our daughter was twelve, I wrote him again asking for him to please meet her. I received a letter from his mother telling me he had his own family and problems of his own, and he really could not be bothered with my child. My daughter began to be very rebellious after that rejection. It was the beginning of her rejection of her stepdad and me.

She had also written to Jim around that time to ask him to meet her. His mother also replied with a terrible rejection letter. She really took it to heart. She became so rebellious that she ended up in a relationship with the wrong young man who was very disrespectful to her and us. She became pregnant at 17 and, of course, she was keeping her baby.

My husband and I tried to talk to her. We told her we would help her with the baby. We knew her boyfriend was not good for her, but she was so in love with him. They got married March of 1995, and our granddaughter was born in August. My granddaughter was and still is my sunshine. I had to stand back and watch as my former son in law abused my daughter verbally. He kept her barefoot and pregnant most of their married life. He cheated on her several times, but she just kept forgiving him and taking the abuse.

I watched her go from being a smart student who dreamed of being a teacher to someone who started college and quit several times, because he beat her self-esteem so down. There was never an encouraging word from him to her. She went through so very much. I always stayed close to her, because I loved her and I did not want her to be lost. When she had our oldest grandson, we were not allowed to even be around him, but God had me start praying

Ezekiel 11:19 (Amplified) and I will give them one heart (a new heart) and I will put a new spirit within them: and I will take the stony (Unnaturally hardened) heart out of their flesh, and will give them a heart of flesh (sensitive and responsive to the touch of their God.)

I prayed that consistently over her. I would put her name in there and cry to the Lord, "Change her heart, Lord, and remind her how much You love her."

Finally I began to see a break in her, and I asked her to go to a meeting where that prophet had first spoken to me. She sat and listened and cried through most of the service. At the end she grabbed my hand and we went forward together. He came to her and spoke a powerful word in her life that changed her forever. He talked about how her stepdad had built her a swing in the back yard and how she used to swing on it and sing to the Lord. At age twelve she just got off that swing and turned her back on God. He told her that the enemy had meant to destroy her, but the Lord had come to rescue her. He told her it was her choice. Then he told us that the enemy had put a wedge between us and had tried to destroy our relationship, but God said He was restoring everything that the enemy had stolen from us. She was saved and filled with the Holy Spirit that night.

Because she started walking with the Lord, it seemed like things got tougher for her in her marriage. The Lord did restore our relationship. She has continued to walk out her salvation, not always perfect, but who of us can even say we are perfect? She has had to face some pretty hard struggles I know I would not have been able to face.

My daughter continued to write to her father through the years but still, there was no response from him. In 2003 when she was pregnant with her fourth child, she had lots of pain in her heart and needed to bring closure to that area of her life.

I started praying again around October, and the Lord told me to write to Jim one more time. This time, I decided not to tell my daughter that I was going to write him. It was hard because we have always told each other everything concerning her father. I felt that this time, God would have to intervene for us to get Jim to respond. He must have heard the cries of my heart because a week later when I went to get my mail, there was a letter from him. My daughter happened to be in the car with me when I picked it up. I said, "Oh my goodness, this is from your father." She said, "Oh, Mom, I didn't tell you but I wrote him last week." Then I told her I did too. We sat in the car and read the letter together. His first words were, "Since I received a letter from both of you last week on the same day, I figured it was time for me to meet our daughter."

He said, "He wanted to meet with me first; then we would talk about him meeting her." We met the next week and talked for several hours. He was really shocked that I was not still angry with him. We cleared the air about a lot of things but never really went deep enough to pull all the hurt out of my heart. I think I was still in that place of fearing being rejected by him all over again. I should have been over all that by then but it was really deep inside me. I did not even realize how deep that pain and rejection had buried itself in my heart. I thought I had overcome all of that stuff years before. I found out several weeks later, I was only at the beginning of the journey of healing as far as he was concerned. The Lord was tearing down another wall and layer of my life that I needed to allow him to heal.

A couple weeks after I first talked with Jim, he came to my home to meet our daughter for the first time. I sat across the room and watched them interact with one another. It was amazing to me to see even though this was the first time they actually spent time together in my daughter's 27 years that they acted very similarly. Their body language was similar. They held their hands and sat with their arms in the same position. They even laughed alike. I already knew she had his eyes and eyebrows but the actions to me where somehow amazing. It made me realize how truly awesome God is.

After that, they talked several more times. She met his wife and learned that she had three half-sisters and one half- brother. I was okay with it all for a while but then something stirred up all the deep anger inside me again. I did not understand where it was coming from. I prayed about it constantly in those days but I got no release. I think I was resentful because he did nothing for her for all those years and suddenly, I had to let him into her life and my four grandchildren's lives. It hit me the wrong way when I heard no remorse for what he did to me.

He never said, "I am sorry I left you to raise her by yourself." He never even told her he was sorry for leaving us. It was always just, "I was young, dumb, and stupid." He told us both that when she was six months old the state asked him what his intentions were towards her. He told them he was not going to do anything for her. He basically signed his rights away. I think the fact that he was not sorry for anything was what stirred up all the anger in me again. I lashed out at him, and, of course, that made him angry and shut everything down again for my daughter.

Finally, after a couple of weeks of that anger, I had enough. I cried out to the Lord to help me change and understand what was happening. I had to get in my quiet place with the Lord. When I began to examine my heart, I saw some things I did not even know were there. I thought I had forgiven him but I had only forgiven him to a small degree. I still had so much hurt in my heart because of him it even kept me from trusting my husband as much as I should have.

I had put him behind a wall of iron and blocked him in so I would never have to look at that area again. I did not care that it had thorns and weeds growing in there. I did not care if he was locked in the prison of my walled heart. I saw all of it in the Spirit, and it was so dark and ugly inside that I wanted to run and hide. I felt so much shame because I was holding all this against him. But in my mind, he deserved it because he had hurt me very much.

After finally examining my heart's motives, I knew I was wrong. I knew I had to forgive him and me; I had to let all of it go once and for all. When I allowed the Lord to take me back to those places that hurt, I unlocked that iron gate with His help and allowed Him in that place of my heart. I allowed Him to go in and begin a new work inside me. I think the biggest thing was the Lord saying to me, "Are you willing to share her with him? Are you willing to share your grandchildren with him?" Those were big questions for me to answer and even face at the time.

After much prayer and time with the Lord, I surrendered. Healing began as a process in this area. A few weeks later, I felt it was necessary to meet him one more time so I could apologize. He agreed to come over to my house again. My daughter and I met with him. I told him I was sorry, and I asked him if he would talk with me one more time. He agreed, we went down the street from my home, and sat in his truck to talk.

I told him I was sorry I had gotten angry at him but that I had a lot of pain inside that needed to be healed. I told him I had some deep questions for him, and I really needed the answers. So I asked him the question that troubled me the most for 27 years. Did he love me or did he just use me? I told him, "That is the one thing I need to know more than anything else. It had hurt me so badly because you told me you loved me. Then you walked away like I was nothing. I loved you very much and when you left me, it destroyed my hopes of ever being loved again. I need to know."

He said, "That is so buried in my heart that I don't let anybody in there." I said, "Well, I am asking you to let me in there because I really need to know. I need to be healed. If you loved me, okay, I will accept that and if you did not love me and you just used me, I will accept that too. I just need closure in this area. You could, at least, tell me the truth after all these years." Again he said, "It is so deep in my heart that it hurts, I do not even let my wife into that part of my heart." I said, "I need you to open up and allow me in there this one time."

He said, "Why didn't you find me years ago and tell me all this?" I said, "Jim, I was a scared sixteen-year-old girl who had already been through so much in my life. I did not know how to talk to you, and I did not think you would listen. I thought of myself as fat and ugly back then. I had been molested and raped by my stepfather when I was young and for me to even think anyone would ever like me or love me was something I had thought would never happen." By then, we were both crying. I said, "You were the first boy I had ever kissed and had ever done anything with and so I felt like I had given you everything. But you rejected me and broke my heart; that is why I need to get into your heart to find out the truth."

We were both crying when he said, "How could you think you were not beautiful because you always have been?" He agreed to tell me the truth that had been hidden in his heart for so long. He said, "Yes I did love you; however, because of my circumstances I had to obey my parents. I wanted to go against them so badly but I could not so I chose to just walk away. I thought it was the best thing to do for you and our daughter. I have regretted that many times over the years but you cannot take back the choices you make when you are young. You think your parents are right but later you realize they were wrong when it is too late to go back."

I cried and thanked him for being honest with me. I asked him if we could please part as friends, and he agreed. We hugged and agreed to be friends. I gave him my old Bible at the Lord's direction, praying that the Lord would draw him to it and he would find Him on those pages. We shared our birthdays together that year. The next year, he moved across the country. He really has not had much to do with our daughter the last several years but she is okay with that at this point. Jim's parents both passed away and never met their granddaughter or even wanted too.

Our daughter believes God did what she asked Him to do and if her father wants to know her more, he will find her. At this point, my heart is completely healed in this area. I believe the Lord answered my prayers even more than I could ever imagine. I am so thankful He allowed my heart to be healed and be unlocked from the emotions of that sixteen–year-old girl who was so broken and hurt. He reached down and set me free.

Now, that area of my heart is a beautiful place. There are no more bars of iron surrounding it and no more thorns growing. I can go to that corner now and see only good things. My heart overflows with joy and peace.

Chapter 10

THE RUINS -MY HUSBAND

Woven between the lines of this book is the man who has loved and cherished me for 36 years. Ours is a love story that has been written with many trials, tears, and tribulations. As we forged our way through each season of our lives together, our love has continued to grow despite all the obstacles that we have had to overcome. He has loved me even when I did not know how to love myself. He never saw me as ugly or broken. He has always loved me for who I am and continues to tell me how beautiful I am.

As I began to walk through those seasons of emotional healing, he was right by my side. As I stepped into ministry, he has always encouraged me to be bold and strong for the Lord. When the Lord began to heal my heart, I had to let him heal the scars that I had hidden. I loved my husband so much that I did not even realize I had unforgiveness in my heart for him. This was a painful area but I knew it needed healing from God.

After all the other healings had taken place, I thought I was done. I was finally at rest in the Lord. However, time with the Lord would show me that I had more areas to work on so they could be healed.

As the peace in my heart grew stronger and as joy began to return to my heart, I started walking through some things with the strength of the Lord. At times, my circumstances seemed to overwhelm me. I would feel this great peace inside but the outside was still a roller coaster ride at times. Sometimes, I even found myself wanting to laugh and smile but then my circumstances would overcome me. I wanted to live on the outside what I was feeling on the inside. I continued to keep my guard up out of fear of rejection.

Many times, as the Lord brought me to another wall, I would think it must be the last one. However, deep inside, I knew there was so much more to face before it was complete. I was in denial. I had built up wall after wall to protect myself. As time went by, I knew it was time for more change in my heart. I knew I would have to be willing to face another wall. Some walls may have been smaller but at times, they seemed even harder to release to God.

The next wall I faced was unforgiveness for my husband. This one was really hard because I had no idea I had even built a wall up against him. I had some roots of unforgiveness growing against him. There were so many emotions flooding my heart that I did not know how to handle them. I had always had a hard time trusting him. I had already been through a bad relationship with my daughter's father, therefore, in the back of my mind I always thought he would reject me and find someone better.

The first time I met my husband, I was a new mom with a two-month-old baby girl. He was nineteen years old and kind of immature. I met him through his sister whom I befriended on my monthly appointments when I was pregnant with my daughter. She was always talking about her brother Bob and how I needed to meet him. I finally said, "Okay, if you think he will like me."

He took me to the car show and to dinner. We had a good time. When he brought me home, he kissed me goodnight and said he would call me. He never called. Finally, I heard through his sister that he really did not like me. I said, "Okay, well, that's the way my life is." I felt so defeated and believed that no one would ever love me. I really had no idea what I wanted in a man other than I wanted him to love me. I had a lot of wrong thinking in my head as a result of being sexually abused when I was a child.

I had turned my back on the Lord for two reasons: the church rejected me and because of my daughter's father.

I felt like I had failed God in so many ways. I decided that if anyone ever did come along I would just give myself to the lust of the flesh because I thought no one would ever love me for me. Deep inside, I tried to have hope but it was just a glimmer.

When my daughter was seventeen months old, my friend called and told me her brother wanted to go out on a date again. I agreed. This time, we went to Worlds of Fun with his family. After we dropped his family off, he brought me home. I liked him for the attention he gave me. We sat in his van, and he wanted to take the kissing a little too far but I stopped him because I already had one child without a daddy, and I sure was not ready for another.

My thinking back then was that I would have to give him what he wanted or I would never keep him. I had no idea there was another way. The only thing I had been taught was not to talk about any of those things. You simply did what you had to and do your best not to get caught.

We went on a roller coaster ride of lust and passion for a year. By this time in my life I had given up on the church and believing God even loved me or my daughter. After all, the church had rejected my daughter and me. My Sunday school teacher ridiculed me one Sunday in front of all the girls in the class when I went back to church with my daughter who was about one year old at the time. I left there feeling ashamed and condemned. I felt at that point there was no hope of ever being loved or forgiven by the Lord. I felt abandoned by the church and all my friends.

So I set out on this road of dating Bob. We thought we were in love but it was more, we were also in lust. Deep inside, those scars drove me to give him what he wanted thinking it would make him love me. After a year of dating, he asked me to marry him. We both were too immature to understand that being married was different from dating.

On August 15, 1979, we got married at the church that I had first gotten saved in. The pastor agreed to conduct a quiet ceremony because he knew me. Only a few people attended because my grandma had said it was shameful for me to be married in a traditional way since I had a baby out of wedlock. My grandma refused to attend the ceremony. That always hurt me so much. She would not even let me take my daughter to my little wedding.

Nevertheless, my family and his threw us a surprise reception later that day. My aunt and uncle were kind enough to let us go down to their lake cabin at Truman Damn for a week. However, Grandma made me take my daughter with us on our honeymoon because she didn't believe I was ever supposed to leave her. We had a wonderful time taking walks and going fishing with our little girl.

We were so happy at first — so much in love with each other. He loved my little girl like she was his own. Sometimes, we fought over discipline but we were fine in the beginning. We moved into his apartment. Since my daughter was only two, many people complained about her crying. The walls were thin and the neighbors could hear everything because there were wooden floors and two-year-olds run a lot. We had to move back in with my grandma.

That was the beginning of our many fights. Bob had a hard time understanding why I had to give my daughter so much attention. I know he felt that way because he was immature. He was so good to my daughter and loved her so much but still had a hard time. My grandma also loved my daughter very much and spoiled her. Grandma did not like it when my husband corrected my daughter.

It was a hard situation to be in. Grandma caused a lot of fights between us. He would run to his family and friends who were influencing him to get away from me. That caused a lot of arguments between us. It became so unbearable that we finally separated a few months later and then divorced. We remained friends and he would come over to see us all the time.

Finally, I told him to stop coming over and to just leave me alone. I still loved him deep inside, and I know he loved me but I thought it would never work between us. My grandma had talked so badly about him that I believed her. She had convinced me that I did not need anyone but her and my daughter.

I was so confused and angry inside that I didn't know what to believe. I just wanted to be left alone. I thought everyone had abandoned me. I set out on a road of partying, smoking, and doing some stupid things. After about six months, I was sick of that lifestyle.

Around Christmas that year, Bob came to see us. I watched as he held my daughter lovingly. He brought her a gift and she was so excited to see him. Something in my heart began to change. I realized that my baby girl needed her momma. I got down on my knees one cold winter's night in January 1981 in my bedroom and cried out to the Lord to forgive me. I did not get up from that place until I felt His presence. I told the Lord that night if I was going to come back to Him then it was going to be forever. I made a commitment to Him but I also made a covenant with Him for life.

When I got up from that floor, I went to my closet and grabbed my Bible from the shelf. I dusted it off, opened it and began to read the book of John until I fell asleep.

I worked at nights at a convenience store, and I took my Bible with me. When I had no customers I read it. The Word became life to me and God began to change my heart.

I tried to go back to my church I had gotten saved and baptized when I was young, but I was judged and ridiculed. They would not accept my daughter or me. No one would even speak to me. I could feel them staring at us. I sat through the service and at the end, the Lord spoke to me and said, "Get your daughter, walk out of this place, shake the dust from your feet and never look back." That is what I did.

I spent the next 6 months pouring over my Bible and praying. As I read the Word, the Lord began to work on my heart towards my husband. The Lord knew me from the beginning and He always knew my heart's desire was to be married and have a family. I listened to Him and repented of all my sins against my husband. I promised the Lord I would ask Bob to forgive me when I saw him again. When you make a promise to the Lord He makes sure you keep it.

In May of that year, Bob came into the store to see me. We had not seen or spoken to each other since Christmas. It was good to see him. As we talked, I began to share with him what had taken place in my life. He listened and wanted to know more. After work, I took him over to my brother's house where my sister- in- law and brother shared the Lord with him also. We asked each other for forgiveness for all we had done or said to hurt each other. Together, we led him to the Lord. I was so happy when I went home that night.

I prayed for him and realized at that moment how much I really loved my husband and how wrong I had been. I knew I had allowed the Enemy to steal the one person God had given me who really did love me. He started coming to see me almost every night. It was wonderful to have that healing take place. I finally decided that I was going to tell him that I really loved him, and I wanted to remarry him if he would have me back.

The next evening he drove up on his new motorcycle. He was so proud of that thing. After my shift was over, I poured my heart out to him and asked him to remarry me. He looked me straight in the eyes and said, "I really do not love you anymore." He then told me that he had moved on and wanted someone new in his life. I said okay and left to go home. I told him it was really not necessary to come see me every night. I went home and cried myself to sleep. I prayed as I cried and told the Lord all my sorrows.

My heart was broken again. This time, it was my fault, and I deserved what I received. Towards the end of my shift the next day, he showed up again. He told me as he prayed, the Lord told him I was the one He had made for him. The Lord told him there would never be another one for him. He asked me to forgive him and said he wanted to remarry me. He told me he had always loved me but was just afraid that we would let family and friends interfere again. I promised him that we would only listen to the Lord this time. We were married two weeks later on July 2, 1981. My family and friends thought we were crazy, and I think his did too but we did not care. They told us that we didn't make it six months the first time and that it will never last this time. God knew we were meant for each other and He knew that it would last.

As a young couple with a child already built into the marriage we had struggles. We made up our minds that with the Lord's help we would be a family. We had committed our lives to the Lord, and we had determined to not give up on each other again. He already loved my daughter and treated her like his own. We lived with my grandma for a few months. She started trying to cause problems again between us but this time, I refused to let her interfere with our relationship. I had never disobeyed my grandma but my marriage came first.

I listened to the Lord and asked my brother if we could move in with his family for a while until we could save enough money to get our own apartment. He agreed to let us and we lived with them for 6 months.

We went through so much those first months. We did fight a lot but we always made up and forgave each other. We made a promise to each other that we would never go to bed angry. For 36 years now we have pretty much kept that promise. When we got our first apartment, we were really happy. We also found a church that accepted us, and we got involved there. We were there every time the doors were open. I loved being a wife and mother, and I really enjoyed my home.

Even though things were good most of the time, there was still a measure of resentment built up in my heart against my husband. I think one of the things that hurt me was that I wanted more children so much. In February 1983 when I found out I was pregnant, we were so excited but I ended up losing the baby. I was very brokenhearted. My husband really did not know how to comfort me, so I pushed him away.

I felt worse when we went to counseling with our pastor; his words broke my heart even more. He told us we would be better off not to have any children and we needed to stop trying to keep up with our friends. Then he said the Lord really did not want us to have any more children. At first, my husband listened to him.

I went home that night and cried so hard. My husband said, "Let us pray about all this," and I agreed. As we prayed, my heart pain lifted but I still built up a wall in my heart to protect myself.

I also resented the fact that my husband wanted me to be his maid. He went to work, came home, and I was supposed to pick up after him, fix dinner, and do everything. Plus, I was supposed to show him love and affection. I got so tired of it and finally, one day I had enough. He came home and started dropping his clothes as he walked in the door with his greasy boots. That night as we fought over him leaving his stuff everywhere, I grabbed his boot and threw it across the room at him, breaking the clock that hung on the wall, barely missing his head. He ran out of the apartment until I cooled off. He came back and apologized.

We agreed we would talk more about things like that. He changed and began to pick up after himself. We were okay but deep in my heart I still felt as if I was just his maid..

We were good where the Lord was concerned. I had to always be in control of everything though because I felt that if I was not, my husband would not take care of me. This thinking came from my childhood. I never had anything much that was mine. We were always moving from place to place. Most of the time, my things would get thrown away. I felt if I didn't control everything, I would lose it all and so, I held on to everything tightly. The problem was, I did not know how to trust Bob. I think I really believed he just loved me because of sex. I had so much wrong thinking back then. After what I went through as a child, I can see why I thought that way.

After a year in the apartment we had to move back in with my grandma because he was not working. That was a very difficult period of our marriage because my grandma did not like my husband correcting my daughter.

In November of 1983, we found out I was pregnant again. Since I had some problems with the last pregnancy, I quit my job and stayed at home.

In June of the next year, the doctor said the baby was breech. It was too late for him to turn because he was due in a few weeks. When I told my husband, he said it would be okay. That night, we went to prayer meeting but I said nothing. At the end, a man named Joel Schneider looked at me and said, "You need prayer. The baby is breech, and you have an Rh blood problem. We are going to pray, and God is going to heal you."

It seemed like nothing happened when they prayed but as we sat in bed reading the Bible together, my husband reached over to put his hand on my tummy, talking to the baby. All of a sudden, we watched as our son turned around in my stomach and got in position to be born. We both started praising the Lord! I will never forget going to the doctor the next week and how amazed he was that the baby had turned. When our son was born, I had no blood issues at all, and his birth was perfect. God had answered.

Becoming a momma again was so wonderful, and I got very busy with my children. We finally got another apartment and my husband got another job. We were a family and happy, or so I thought. I wore myself out just trying to keep up and started babysitting to help with finances. That put more stress on me. I was sick a lot but I kept pushing myself.

When our son was 10 months old we went on our first family vacation to California to see my mom and brothers. I had not seen my older brother for eleven years. We had a lot of fun traveling across the country in a little Datsun with two kids. We barely had enough money to get home but this is one of our family's special memories. When our son was seventeen months old we were able to finally purchase my grandma's home. By then she was living with my aunt and uncle in Kansas. It felt so good to be back in my childhood home. I settled down to raise my family. However I was totally exhausted from babysitting and felt like I was going to have a break down. So I gave up babysitting to concentrate on my family.

That same year, my husband decided to adopt my daughter. She was so happy to finally have the same last name as her momma. My husband had been around her since she was seventeen months old. He was the only daddy she ever knew. She loved him as much as he loved her.

On my second trip to California to visit my mom and brothers, I had a feeling when I was out there that I was pregnant and sure enough, I was. Bob and I were both excited to find out we were expecting again — at first. As the pregnancy progressed, my husband seemed to grow distant. The busyness of life caused us to neglect praying together and reading the Word. We were growing apart but I did not see it. I just kept pushing myself to be everything for everybody.

Bob started going for walks with the kids soon after he found out I was pregnant. I didn't think anything about it but then, one night, he told me he saw a former neighbor who had lived in the apartment building we lived in years before. He said she was divorced now and worked at the donut shop up the street. I said, "Oh, so that's where you have been walking to." He said, "Yeah, once in a while." I said, "Oh, okay," not thinking anything about it.

Then he started disappearing at nights for hours. I had enough, and we got in a huge fight. I told him it was her or me but I was not going to be second fiddle to anyone. I told him if he was planning to cheat on me, he had better walk out the door right now. I would never ever put up with a man who cheats. He walked out the door and told me he was leaving me. I said, "Okay, go ahead but you will be sorry." He took off walking down the street, and I closed the door behind him.

Grabbing my babies in my arms, I just hugged them and went on doing my work. I stopped and cried for a few minutes and got them ready for their baths and bed. After I put them to bed, I sat on the couch, cried, and talked to the Lord about all of it.

After a while he came back and asked to come in. I told him to just get his stuff and go.

He said, "No, I cannot go because the Lord will not let me."

I said, "What are you talking about?"

He said, "I was going to leave you but the Lord stopped me in my tracks and reminded me of what He had told me years before. He told me that it would be the biggest mistake I ever made because you were the only one for me. He made you for me, and if I left you, there would never be another who loved me like you."

He was crying and begging me to forgive him. I did forgive him but another wall went up, and I still did not trust him. For years after that, every time he was late, I worried he was cheating on me.

When our second son was born we were so happy. We were a growing family. When our second son turned one, I found out I was pregnant again. My husband had already told me he did not want any more children so he was not happy. This caused me so much stress, and I was sick throughout the pregnancy.

While I was pregnant, he decided that he was going to take care of that problem of not having anymore children, and he did. I was so hurt when he decided to do that. He pushed me into agreeing to it because he wanted it. I was trying to please him but inside, my heart was broken. I really wanted more children, and he knew that. I also had to listen to people who said, "Do you know what causes that?" Or the ones that said, "You are so poor now; how can you have another baby?" My heart broke every time I heard someone say anything bad about my family.

I was so stressed when I had our third son that both our lives were in danger. Many doctors were in the delivery room with me. Even the pediatrician was there. They were waiting for our son to be born because he was overdue and he was having some issues. As soon as he was born, I heard him cry. They rushed him out of the room to work on him. When the doctor looked at me, I rolled my eyes back in my head and began to hemorrhage. They threw the bed back and got me stabilized. In the meantime our son was being worked on too.

God was good to both of us and allowed us to live. My son was healthy but I was not well. I had lost a lot of blood but back then, they were afraid to give transfusions. The doctor said, "Go home; take it easy, and you will build your blood back up." Problem was I had no one to help me with four children. My husband just thought I could go back to doing everything I did before. Our son was born in late October and my strength really never came back.

By the time January came along I was really sick with flu-like symptoms. I was bleeding and could not keep anything down; I did not have the strength to raise my head off the pillow. I went into the hospital, and my children were spread out to church families who were willing to help.

They did not know what was wrong with me so after a week, they isolated me. The nurses were so scared of me they would not even come in and help.

After another week of that, I knew if I did not fake being well, I would not get out of there. They sent me home and my husband insisted the kids all come home. I went right back to being mom but the problem was I was still sick. I was home a week and then had to go back to another hospital where I was treated much better.

Again, my children were sent out to families willing to help us. I spent two more weeks in the hospital but when I came home, I went right back to work as mom again. I lived in pain every day of my life pretty much. I did not know how to just stop and rest. I had to do it all. My kids were the reason I got up in the mornings and why I fought so hard to be well.

I spent the next three and a half years pushing myself and living in pain every day. I was in and out of the hospital. One day, in the late summer of 1992, they put me in the hospital and could not get my body to turn around. I lay on that bed for a month barely able to raise my head off the pillow. Finally, I was given a choice to either go home and die or to have surgery. I chose surgery because I wanted to live for my husband and children.

On the day of my six and half hour surgery, my husband never left that hospital. He stayed by the intensive care all night sleeping in a chair. I think he realized that he almost lost me that day. They said my recovery would be long but God said, "No it will not."

I was released from the hospital in one week. The day I came home, I did not tell my husband. I had my mom take me home. I first surprised my middle son who was five at the time. He came running into my arms and gave me a huge hug and kiss. Then my mom drove me home to my other three children. When I stepped out of the car they all came running. The three-year-old had his arms out wide screaming, "Mommy!"

My husband was so surprised when he came home and saw me. He was very caring and loving to me. We struggled with a few issues but for the most part, he finally realized I could not carry the load I had been carrying for so long. Through all the baseball, dance recitals and everything involved in raising children, I was very thankful the Lord had allowed me to stay and be with my family.

In 1997 my husband wanted to move across the country to California. He was tired of the job he had for fourteen years. We put our home up for sale and when it finally sold in July, we packed up all our belongings in a U-Haul. We headed for California with three boys and a small dog. Our sons had to give away their German shepherd that they loved. We said goodbye to our daughter and granddaughter, which broke my heart. We also said goodbye to family and friends of many years.

However, we were so excited thinking we were on a great adventure. It turned out to be exactly that. When we got there, we stayed with my mom in her mobile home at a retirement village. Those people complained all the time about our boys, even though they rarely went outside.

My husband got a job a couple of weeks later and it seemed like a great opportunity. We used our savings as a down payment on a new home and moved in. I set up our home beautifully. We lived there about two weeks when my husband came home and said, "I got fired." I was shocked. It was the last thing I expected.

We decided to move out of the house because we had not signed the papers yet. We moved back in with my mom and put our things back into storage. My husband looked for work but could find none. We then decided to return to Missouri. We waited for his retirement savings to come and cashed what we thought would get us home. After giving away more of our things, we packed the truck again, told my mom goodbye, and headed home to Missouri. We managed to get as far as New Mexico before we ran out of gas and money and had to sleep in the truck that night at a truck stop.

I used a pay phone to call the manager of our bank in Missouri and begged him to deposit the check he had in his hand into our then closed account. In tears, I explained our situation. He finally agreed to reopen our account and deposit the check giving us access to the money so we could get home. We were tightly packed in that U Haul but we made it even with our little dog. At one point, the dog even set off the fire extinguisher. We all laughed about that but I knew it was going to be hard going back. We had no home to go to and no jobs. We had to live with our daughter's family. It was hard because they lived in a small apartment on the third floor.

After a couple of weeks, the people living downstairs started to complain about too much noise. My husband tried to find a job but had problems. He was finally hired by a friend but it would only be for a short while. Our boys had to live with one of our daughter's friends for about three weeks then she said she was going to call DFS on us. It is so strange how people say they want to help but what they really want to do is cause issues.

Finally, we found a rental house. We could not put it in our name so we had to use the names of our son-in- law and daughter. We used all of our savings and rented that place so we could all live together again. It was November, just before Thanksgiving.

I watched my granddaughter while her parents worked. Christmas that year was so depressing. My husband's job was not going too well and he was telling me that it would not last too much longer.

I decided in January the following year to look for a job because his job was ending. I found one but the stress was not good for me because of my health. I had a colostomy bag on my side and sometimes, it would detach itself from me. Stress was usually the cause. I had to explain that to my employer, which for the most part one of the managers understood. Several days, I had to leave work and run home to change it.

One night, the other manager was there and right at closing time, I realized it was coming off. I still needed to count my drawer down and straighten up the store. I went to the manager and told him I needed to leave. He asked me why, and I told him. He yelled at me, told me to get my stuff, get out of the store and never come back. He said he had someone else who had one of those; it came off and made a mess everywhere.

I was so broken and hurt. I went home and cried, feeling so helpless and unable to help my husband with finances. He tried to understand but for the most part he did not. I think I needed compassion but he did not feel that for me at the time. He was so stressed out himself that he didn't realize what I was going through. His lack of consideration and compassion at that time created another wall and feelings of resentment.

Then the IRS took our income tax by mistake, and we had to work our way out of that mess. By the end of January, my husband finally found a job.

Without even asking what had happened, our daughter got angry, called her husband and their friends and told them I had quit my job. Our son-in-law came home with his friend and his wife ran in the other room grabbed the baby and our daughter, and rushed them out of the house.

My sons watched in horror as my son- in- law and his friend confronted me. They put their fist in my face and were going to hit me but something stopped them. They told us to get out of their house. Our daughter sat in the car and called the police on her own parents. I woke up my husband and told him what happened. He never defended me. He just said, "Get in the car. Let's go." It hurt so much that he did not stand up for me.

We left there with our son-in-law threatening to throw all our things in the trash. We had no place to go. It was a scary thing to know that we were now homeless. But God was watching out for us. That night, we stayed with a friend and her children. The Lord reminded me of an offer some of our friends made a few months before. They had offered to let us stay in their basement if our housing situation got to be too much. I called them and the offer was still open.

Praise God! We had somewhere to stay until we could get on our feet again. Our friends were so good to us to take in a family of five and a dog. But those days in that basement were challenging. We lived there for nine months. I had a gallbladder attack while living there and a major asthma attack. I ended up in the hospital both times. I tried to go to work after the gallbladder surgery but just could not handle it.

At first, I was very depressed about living there but then I decided to make the best of it. I made that little area a home as much as I could. My husband was very withdrawn at this time. We lost lots of the important things we did as a family, like sitting down to dinner together. Our lives were so consumed by trying to survive and get out of that basement. I felt like such a failure as a parent. We lost our car because we could not afford to pay for it. Fortunately, a friend gave us an old beat up car so my husband could get to work.

We were attending another church by then, and I was really trying to fit in again. I remember sitting in the pew and no one would even talk to me. We had been going there for several weeks by then. I remember telling the Lord that if no one came and talked to me that night, I would never return. About that time, a woman sat beside me and asked me my name. Then she asked if I needed prayer, and I told her, "Yes, my family is homeless."

She said, "Oh my! I know you because you are the family we have been praying for at our weekly Bible study."

I thought, "Lord, you did hear me and you answered." I started going to those Bible studies for several months. It helped me to make it through that time.

We had to give away more of our things and bring the rest to our friend's garage. My heart ached to have my own place but I had to wait. My dad and stepmom even came to see us while we were living there. They never offered to help us get out of there though. One night, as we tried to get rid of more of our things, the people who hosted the Bible study at their house just showed up in the driveway. They handed us a check for one thousand dollars so we could get our own place. My heart was so happy. Our friends had been telling us for a few weeks it was time to move on. We had saved just a little bit of money. Feeding three boys and living on such a small income was really hard.

Most of our so called "friends" judged and condemned us for being homeless. We ended up finding a small two-bedroom home that we could afford. We made it our home and learned how to be a family again. We still felt the loss of something but I could not explain it. We lived in that home for five years until the land lady said she was selling it and we had to move.

After my son- in- law threw us out of their house that we had used all our money to get it was hard on me. I wanted to see my granddaughter so one day when he was not home I went to see her. I just showed my daughter love like I had always done in the past. It really hurt her brothers because they could not see their sister or niece. Our sons were eight, ten, and thirteen at the time. It took a long time to get over the pain all of that caused.

Our daughter had our first grandson that July, and she did not even call us until the next day. When we went to see him, we were treated like we were unwelcomed and unwanted. I was very hurt. All my husband said was, "Just let it go. Let her do what she wants." He did not stand up for me. I was hurt again.

I continued to build walls against my husband. I felt he put so much on my shoulders and that I always had to make all the decisions. When I finally slowed down and began to actually look at the brick walls that separated us, I was totally ashamed of myself. He had really done the best he knew how.

After moving to our next house, I thought all our problems were over but it seemed like they got worse. We really had no time to look for a place, and I wanted to own a home. My husband would not lead me in any way. He would not say what we should or should not do. So I took it upon myself to find a house for our family. I finally found one but it needed a lot of work. We decided to buy it even though the payment was a bit higher than we had been paying in rent. I thought we could make it. The people who owned the house helped us quite a bit. I really think they wanted it off their hands.

We moved there in July 2003. I thought we had finally settled, and I could be happy. Well, it ended up being a big headache. We struggled to make ends meet. As soon as we paid off the debt for the other car we bought, the transmission went out. Life was just one struggle after another. The payment for the house got to be too much so we refinanced but the payment was even higher. We had so many medical bills we could not keep up. The utilities were really high at the house and we sank deeper and deeper into debt.

When the bank was going to foreclose on us, we declared bankruptcy and were going to keep our home. My mom came to live with us for a year, and we did okay because she was helping us. Then she decided to leave, and we could not make the payment again. They were going to foreclose again. They told us to get out, so we did. We moved into my friend's house and that was hard on everyone. My dad gave us money to get a small duplex. Again, we gave away everything and felt very overwhelmed.

The mortgage company could not decide what they were doing or what the payment was going to be. Then they told us to move back in, so we did. We lived there another four years before they finally told us we had to move. We had no way to save money because the utilities and taxes were eating up every extra cent we had.

In 2009, I was rear-ended and had to have back surgery because of it. I ended up in a lawsuit against my insurance company because they did not want to pay. After two years, we finally settled. I took most of that money and bought us a home with my dad helping with half of it. He told me at the time it was part of my inheritance but he wanted to be paid back. People would always ask me, "How is that an inheritance?" We did okay paying him for the first couple of years but then our insurance would no longer pay for my medical supplies. I could no longer pay my dad, so he had me make quilts for everyone he could think of. My heart has always been heavy about this because when my step-mom passed away, he made several promises and then took most of them back. I watched him give her daughter an eleven thousand-dollar truck and never asked for money back. Again my husband never stood up for me. He just let me go through all the hurt by myself.

We moved into this house and remodeled the entire place, spending the last of our money. We actually have done pretty well here. We have struggled at times but for the most part, we have been okay. My dad refuses to allow us to sell this home until he dies. He says that's his way of making sure we have a place to stay. Our heart's desire has always been to get out of the city and move to the country. Maybe after my husband retires, it will be possible.

I think it took me so long to forgive my husband and allow the walls to be torn down because things just kept happening. I had to learn how to trust the Lord and lean upon Him in all things. Then after I forgave my husband, I had to learn how to trust him again.. The Lord had to teach me that my husband was different, and I needed to learn how to listen and trust him. When I finally learned those necessary lessons, I could go into that part of my heart's garden and be at peace.

I remember falling on my face asking the Lord to heal my marriage. The struggles of life had forced us apart. We allowed a wedge to be put between us. However, the Lord began to heal those wounds one by one. I spent many days crying and healing. The Lord was so good to change my heart and heal all those wounds. We are better today than we were back then. We have a wonderful relationship again. It's not perfect but it is good. God is in the midst of it. We have a wonderful family and are very close.

Many times, people do not understand why we are so close but God put a bond between us that will not be broken.

Two of our children are married. Our daughter is remarried now and has four children of her own and three stepchildren. Our oldest son is married and has three boys and a girl. Our two younger sons are not married yet. We are a blessed family because years ago we made God our source. Yes, we have been through many things in our lives but God has always been so faithful. We will be married 36 years on July 2, 2017. I am so thankful that God gave me the best man He could for me. My husband has loved me even when I could not stand myself. God is so faithful, and He always restores what the Enemy tries to destroy.

Those walls that I allowed to remain were by choice. Maybe it was to protect myself. I know I had to control everything because I feared not being taken care of. He also made some really bad choices that hurt me

I thought there just could not be any walls against my husband, but time spent with my Prince of Peace showed me that I had unforgiveness in my heart towards him. I chose to only give him a small portion of my heart, but deep inside I feared him leaving me for another.

When I came to that wall I realized how ugly it really was. I was holding things against him, and many of them I did not even realize. I poured my heart out to the Lord and He forgave me. The Lord healed our marriage completely. God is in control of all things and He wanted us restored.

Our marriage is a testimony to the Lord of how He can take two people who were not walking with Him and save them. Then He restored their marriage. We are a blessed family because the Lord put His hand on us years ago when we were young.

When I looked back on that wall, I thought to myself how silly it was to even have it there. It was because of a lot of fear and rejection in my past. Fear can make you do some very strange things.

My husband is a diamond in the rough because he has always loved me for who I am and who God made me to be. He has always seen me as his gift from God. We have lived our vows of "for sickness and health, richer and poorer" but God has always walked us through and been faithful. That place in my heart is so beautiful now. We are truly friends forever as the Lord always wanted us to be.

Chapter 11

LEARNING ABOUUT THE LITTLE FOXES
THAT SPOIL THINGS

Have you ever planted a garden? For it to grow, you have to tend it on a daily basis. Over time, if it is taken care of, it becomes a beautiful place to rest and find peace. It is the same with our heart's garden; in order for it to become a beautiful place, it must be tended to daily by Jesus' loving and caring hands.

My heart's garden became a place of war. The ground was covered with broken down walls and gates. There were weeds and thorn bushes growing everywhere. There was no order or balance in my heart's garden for a very long time, except in that one very small corner I had allowed my Prince of Peace to attend.

The rebuilding of my heart's garden began almost immediately after the walls began to be torn down. As I started that journey, I realized I had to surrender all my will to God. Because I so longed to be free, I made that choice to trust Him. In everyone's life we have a choice either to ignore God's pleading to come closer to Him or we choose to hear His voice and obey.

That day, as I stood at that gate, my choice was to surrender to His will, not mine. I had to walk up to many walls and face them. I am so thankful to say that even though I ran for a while from some of them, I eventually returned.

While He had me facing each of those walls and surrendering my will to His will, He was busy rebuilding my heart's garden. My Prince of Peace wanted me to be able to walk in my gardens with love, joy, and peace. He did not want me to walk in fear of anything any longer because His perfect love cast away all fear.

His rebuilding has been a work of love and care that still goes on to this day because the Enemy still tries to plant seeds of destruction in my garden. The difference now is that my Prince of Peace comes and takes His sword of truth and tears down the untruths right away because I have given Him full reign of my heart's garden.

As I stood in that garden area on that first day that was perfect, looking out at the rest of my garden areas, all I could see was brokenness. I turned around to see my Prince of Peace walking towards me. As I ran into His arms He stopped to embrace me with His love.

As he embraced me, He whispered in my ear, "I love you." Then He looked me in my eyes with so much love and compassion and said, "We must begin to rebuild your gardens now.

"He took my hand in His, and we began our journey of rebuilding those gardens that had been destroyed by the Enemy. As I looked around, all I saw were ruins in every direction. Walls of ruins of fear, doubt, and unbelief stood before me in every direction. Before time began, the Prince of Peace saw the finished project and decided that I was worth the time it would take to rebuild my heart's garden. Each day, He gave me the strength to walk through all the destruction that faced me.

During those first days of rebuilding, I would run to Him and cry out for Him to help me walk through those walls of pain I felt. It gave me strength to know I could run into His arms at any moment that I needed to.

Like a good gardener my Prince of Peace began to till up that hard rocky ground with his spiritual spade of love. He turned the soil of untruths and began pulling out every weed that had been planted there. Matthew 15: 13 says that He will take out all the things by the root, which have been planted in our hearts that are not from God.

Everything that had robbed me in the past from seeing the truth of who I am and how much He loves me He pulled out by the root.

That tilling of the soil hurt very much at times. It was very uncomfortable and even embarrassing because I let myself to believe so many lies that the Enemy had planted to destroy my life. Those lies kept me in bondage of fear, doubt, and unbelief.

Little Things about Grandma & Grandpa

One of the things I always believed in my life was that I was a burden to my grandma and grandpa. They were very poor people and for them to take me in I know was a great burden. Although they did their best to care for me all my life, it was a struggle. My grandma was a really hard woman at times and very hard on me. She always said unkind, hard words to me. It took me a long time to realize she was treating me the way she had been treated as a girl. Still, it was hard being told, "You're as big as a barrel at 7 and 8 years old." That continued into my adult life. She put me in a girdle when I was 8 thinking it would slim me down. I was really never encouraged by my grandma or grandpa either. They never attended anything I did at school so I was not motivated to try hard because I felt no one cared anyway. My grandpa had this attitude that women were just to be men's servants.

They were both very heavy drinkers. Back then you could take children in the bars. Because I was my grandpa's tag along, he would take me with him. He would sit me up on the bar and all the old guys would buy me Shirley Temples. When my mom left me at 9 years old, they were only allowed to do that for a short time longer. The laws changed and for many reasons, I was really glad. It was so scary at times riding home at 2:00 AM when my grandpa had finished drinking.

We always seemed to make it though. The hardest time was Christmas and my birthdays because there was never anything under that tree for me. I hoped and prayed something would come for me. My mom would always promise to send me something but nothing ever came. Christmas was also hardest because my cousins, aunts, and uncles came over. My cousins would show me their new stuff. I had nothing.

I was the one kid who was never allowed to go play with the children in the neighborhood most of the time. My grandpa had a hard time letting me have any friends at all. I can remember having just two pairs of jeans and three shirts for school. I got one new pair of shoes each year. They struggled just to pay their bills. When I came to live with them, they stopped going out and started drinking at home on the weekends.

I stayed in my room a lot and played with the two dolls I had been able to keep and my two Barbie's my dad sent me one Christmas when my mom had me. I started at a young age making my own Barbie clothes out of my grandma's scrap bucket. I spent so much time alone that I talked to myself just so I would have a friend. I also talked to Jesus all the time.

In spite of the sad times, there were some good times too. My grandpa always tucked me in at night with snuggle kisses and loves. He would brush my hair 100 times every night. I never went to bed hungry, and I had a roof over my head. I actually thought that was what I deserved because I was lucky I was taken in — as I was told many times by my grandma. I was taught how to take care of myself and to show respect for my elders for sure.

I never realized that the little things were issues in my heart until at one point, the Lord showed them to me. He explained that these things were like little foxes that spoil everything. He said they could grow into big things if I did not allow them to be healed in my heart. So at that point because I wanted healing and my heart to be swept clean, I allowed the Lord to till up all those old wounds I had buried deep inside. The Lord took His time bringing up all the hurt. Yes, I cried, because I loved my grandparents so much for giving me a home. I realized though that I had never forgiven them for things they had said and done. It was very hard to go back to those places of pain because I did not want to remember. By this point, they had both passed. But after it was all said and done, I was thankful I had walked back to those hurtful places and forgiven them and myself for believing I was supposed to be treated that way.

Little Cracks in My Armor

Nevertheless, there were more little foxes in my life spoiling my vine that I needed my Prince of Peace to work on. At those times when it was so painful my Prince of Peace would stop His work and take me again in His loving arms, embracing me in His love. He would whisper in my ear, "Dance with Me, My love." As we danced through out those gardens of pain and fear I rested myself in those loving arms. His love would surround and fill me so that I could go on allowing Him to take that spade of love and till up that old soil.

After He tilled up that soil and pulled out all the thorns and weeds, He brought in some rich black soil, which is the word of God. At first He started with one or two scriptures to help me stand on the truth. He would take that spade of love and mix the word with what He had already planted in my garden.

As he mixed the rich soil into my heart's garden I began to grow stronger. He wanted me to be immoveable when the storms of life came at me. My heart's garden became full of strong oak trees planted in the soil by His living water. They became immoveable to the plots and plans of the enemy.

My strength became Him and the rich soil of His word that He continued to stir up in my garden. With every scripture He planted in my garden I became rooted deeper and deeper in His love and the truth of His love for me. Many times in the process of planting the truth in my heart's garden He sent some fertilizer to help it grow more truth. The fertilizer came from others who were sent into my path to speak a word of encouragement into my life.

That fertilized word would then be added to that rich black soil of the Word and stirred together to make me stand stronger. He pulled out those negative words and replanted the new words that had been spoken to me. These new words helped me to change and grow into the woman He wanted me to be, There were many times where I had to allow Him to dig down deep into those rooted words and things in my past. As I allowed Him access to those things, He could pull them out and replant new words of truth.

As my Prince of Peace pieced those words of truth together I continued to grow stronger. Faith and hope seeds were planted everywhere in my garden and the buds began to spring up everywhere. Even when it looked so bleak on the outside in the natural world, my heart's garden was budding with hope, love and truth.

The Holy Spirit's rain would come down, watering it, comforting me in the hard times and strengthening me through all the pain of pulling out the weeds. At times the Holy Spirit's rain came in a drenching flood. At those times, I stood in the midst of my heart's garden with my arms outstretched, with His light shining on my face, and bask in His loving presence.

It was at these times that my Prince of Peace took me in His loving embrace and whispered in my ear, "Dance with Me, My love." As we waltzed together in those gardens, peace overwhelmed my soul. It was as if every part of me was being saturated in His loving presence. It would flood into every place that was dry and weary in my garden. In the days when I felt weary the Holy Spirit's rain comforted me over and over again. It is a never ending supply.

Wrapped in His presence, my heart's garden filled with His warm sunlight. In those times I had joy bubbling over and unspeakable, for His light flooded into the depths of my soul. He left no area unturned, for my Prince of Peace had set out to bring healing into every area of my life. He knew what each area needed. Nothing could stop His loving hands from piercing into every area, uncovering all the old foundation so He could rebuild new.

In time we went to every area together so that he could heal them all. Some of these places took several years to complete. Many times when I was overwhelmed, He said to me, "There is another day" so we moved on, allowing me to rest in His presence. The more I allowed Him in my garden areas, the more I wanted Him to heal those broken places.

In the beginning it was like I was behind a wall myself, because I had locked all my emotions, my fears and my doubts up and put them in a box on a shelf. It was also because of all the gates and walls I had built to put the abuse behind me. In His time He made each area what He desired them to be. No longer was my heart's garden divided by walls, gates, and "No Trespassing" signs. Now it has become a garden undivided and full of love, for He has healed all the brokenness with His loving hands.

As He kept planting those beautiful words of faith and hope in my heart's garden, they would bloom into wonderful words of encouragement for others. While He was planting those words in me, the enemy continued to use people to plant words of doubt, fear and unbelief in my heart's garden. My Prince was always on guard to take His sword and cut those words down with His love and truth. It was as if there was a little crack in my armor because I would still listen to people. They would say, "You're no good at that," or "God did not call you to do that because I do not see you doing that." "You cannot sing or preach or teach." "You're ugly, fat, stupid." I always attached myself to people I wanted to be like, and I sought their approval.

People and their words always tore me down because they looked on the outside. I was so afraid to speak up to people. I always allowed others to have the last word. I felt like I did not have an opinion or even a voice. I feared what people thought about me every day of my life. They did not look on the inside where God was doing all the wonderful work in my heart's garden.

People always seemed to catch me off guard. It was like I would begin to trust them and then I would let my guard down, thinking they would not hurt me. I truly wanted to believe that all Christians would not hurt me or my family but I found out that Christian people can be very unkind at times. I would think this person would be different but it was always the same. The words would always come until I would be hurt and offended. If I dared question them or got upset, I would always be the one in the wrong even if I was the one hurt by what was said. Every time, I was the one who had to apologize first. Finally, I accepted that I had to learn to just run to the Lord for help.

This area became a huge crack in my armor, until the Lord stepped in and began to close the door on people and their negative words. I had to learn to stand on my own with just Him, and a selected group of friends and family I could trust. I had to stop letting negative people tear me down. Doing so was very hard, because I really wanted friends. It is like He began sealing the doors and that crack in my armor. He then put this shield around me, so that each time they would come at me with their words, those words began to just bounce off my back.

I had to choose to let the Lord close the doors on the ones who kept tearing me down. I had to allow Him to pluck them out of my heart's garden. There have been many people He has put in my life for a season who were supposed to encourage me but they chose to discourage me so He removed them from my life.

This walk has been very lonely at times. The more I allowed those words of doubt and fear to bounce off my back, the more that crack closed up in my wall of armor that surrounds me.

Time has healed the broken places in my heart's garden. My Prince has been faithful to stand guard and take His sword to cut down those words with His love and truth.

In that armor where it was cracked, I would always seem to have this thing. I was not only getting attacked by people's words but I always seemed to continue to go back into abuse situations. Maybe it was because of the tremendous amount of pain I experienced as a child. I kept taking the abuse because, as a child, I had no choice. Even when I grew up I felt like I had no choice but to allow people to abuse me with their words. I thought it was what I was supposed to do in order to be accepted and loved by them.

After many years of being a doormat for people to wipe all their abuse on, I finally had enough and ran into the arms of my Prince of Peace. I asked Him to help me stand up to all those who tried to destroy my life and my peace.

God Has Me

The Lord taught me that I did not need anyone's approval but His. He has taken me in His loving arms, wrapping me in His love, so that whenever anyone tries to come against me with their words,

I know He has me, and I will not fall. I still love them but I know I do not have to stand by and allow anyone to destroy who I am or what God has placed in my heart to do.

On the outside, many people still see me as broken and unfixable. On the inside, the gardener of my life's garden has transformed my heart into a beautiful place just as a caterpillar in a cocoon emerges as a beautiful butterfly. That is what has happened to my heart's garden. That is what He wants for all His children.

Every day now, I sit at His feet knowing He has done a great work in my heart. He has completed His work. I am so thankful for the love and time He has taken with me. Many would have said that I was not worth wasting His time on but I am very thankful He thought I was worth taking the time for.

Do you need healing in your heart's garden? I pray you will allow Him, the Prince of Peace, to walk in those areas of your heart that have been broken.

He longs to be the gardener of your heart so true healing can come to you. He will take His loving hands and till up every area, filling you with His love, faith, and hope. All it takes is your willingness to surrender to Him. Let Him gain access to the areas you have locked up. He longs to fill your heart with peace so you can rest and trust in Him.

Now as I look at my armor, I know He has ridden in on His white stallion and sealed up all the cracks that were there allowing the Enemy access. As I go to my quiet place and run into His arms, He is always waiting for me. We embrace and He kisses my forehead. I look into those wonderful eyes that fill my soul with love. He whispers in my ear, "Dance with Me, My love." As we waltz together, joy floods my heart, knowing I am with the Lover of my soul, my Prince of Peace.

Chapter 12

DIGGING THE WELLS

While all the planting, rebuilding and healing was taking place, there was also a well of living water being dug deep into my heart's garden. These wells were like springs that flowed from the throne room of God.

They were not dug by my Prince; they were dug by me. While I sat at my King's feet one day in my garden, He began to talk to me about digging these wells so that my garden could keep growing. He told me I was only at the beginning stage of what He wanted me to do for Him.

I began to ask Him what the wells were and how I would find them. He told me that the Holy Spirit would be my guide and my teacher. He said all I needed to do was ask Him, and He would show me the way. I had known the Holy Spirit for a long time but I didn't really know Him as my teacher and friend. I had not been down that road of learning yet.

For many years, my relationship with the Lord was superficial. I had no idea there was so much more to knowing and walking with Him. My spirit longed for more. I searched all the time for the truth when I finally discovered, it was so simple and it had been right in front of me all along. I had to repent for my unbelief and for not seeing sooner.

My Superficial Christian Walk

My spirit longed for that true intimate relationship with my King of Kings. I remember always saying there has to be more to this than what I see and believe. There is so much more to gain than what we see on the surface. Matthew 6:33 says, "Seek ye first the kingdom of God and all His righteousness and all these things will be added unto you." This scripture became my life scripture because I longed in my spirit to know God personally.

Because so many of my Christian years were superficial, I would go to my prayer time and run down my list of needs and wants that were in front of me, never realizing that there was more to be had with the Lord. Then I would get up thinking I was trusting Him but would always find myself carrying the burden. I was always trying to figure out the problem for the Lord. Always thinking to myself, "It needs to be done by someone." It could have been something as simple as meeting a need at church or teaching a class. Or it could have been that someone had a need for something. I would always pray my little prayer and then get up and say, "Okay, this is what I will do."

In those days, I never learned to be still before the Lord and wait for the answers. Those superficial five-minute prayers were just so I could say I had prayed. Needless to say, I never felt at peace in those times.

Praying the way I did can get you in a lot of trouble because you are not trusting Him. It caused me to make some bad choices in my life. I wanted to control the situation and the outcome. I was afraid to trust the Lord for the outcome. I was afraid that He would not come through for me.

 From the beginning of my walk with the Lord, I was full of worry and fear. I worried and fretted about everyone and everything. I worried about my children to the point of holding myself in bondage. I did not understand that when my husband and I gave each one of them to the Lord before they were even born, they were His. I did not understand that He had chosen and given them to us to nurture and train up in His Word.

I believed the Bible, which says, "Train up a child in the way he should go and when he is old he will not depart from it." We had to let them go out and serve Him. I wanted to love and protect them from everything and everyone who would hurt them.

I think that was because in my childhood, my parents left me and I felt unprotected. I felt they never really cared about me or what happened to me. I made up my mind I would never let my children feel abandoned by me. I poured my life and love into them. That was fine when they were young but when they became older it became very hard to let them go so they could find their own way.

Around that same time, I allowed my Prince out of His captive state, and He began to replant and rebuild my garden. In that process of learning how to trust Him again, He began to teach me how to dig those wells of living water. It was like there were so many being built at the same time but it was the only way for me to learn how to lean on, rely on and trust Him.

Learning to Dig the Wells

I had a well for my husband and each one of my children. When He gave me the tapestry ministry, I dug wells for each one He gave me. The tapestry ministry was one of seeing a vision of a healing quilt and then bringing it to life through material. This ministry has brought so much healing to others as well as to me. The wells were for me to see the promises of truth in God's Word. They were also for me to be able to trust Him with the promise that He does have a plan for each one of their lives. As the wells started flowing upon them, I began to see change coming in their lives. Then I grew and stood stronger on God's Word. I would trust Him more and just stand back and watch as He touched their lives in amazing ways.

I have also seen the wells stop flowing for a while. This always happened when I got too busy with the cares and worries of this life. During those times, I would stop going to my heart's garden, praying, and sitting at my Master's feet. However, He always forgave me for not staying on the task He had assigned me to do. He was always very willing to forgive me by wrapping me in His arms of love. He would hold me in His arms and whisper in my ear, "Dance with Me, My love." As we waltzed together, it seemed as if all those things that I had worried and cried about a few minutes before were all forgotten and forgiven.

The Lord is the keeper of our hearts' gardens but He requires us to do our part too. If we do not do our part, those places He has given us charge over become neglected. He assigned me to dig the wells of prayer, praise, and the Word for my family and others. The wells were the living water of the Word for their lives.

Digging My Well

The first well He told me to dig was for my life because He wanted me to know Him so I could believe in the impossible for others. So on a bright sunny morning in my garden, though cloudy on the outside with no answers to the problems I faced, I ran into His arms crying for Him to please teach me.

That day, as I sat there listening and learning, He taught me how to search the Word and it came to life. I absorbed it in my heart. "Seek ye first the kingdom of God and His righteousness, and all these things will be added to you" (Matthew 6:33).

As I dug in that well of living water I discovered the meaning of each word and the truth that was hidden there. Then I put myself in that word, speaking to myself as the lord would do. I realized that I had just been reading the word and not absorbing it into my spirit with the life it gives.

As I sat and meditated on the word in my garden, I knew I would have to work on this every day. I dug that well deep into the Word. Healing, restoration, break through, and many more words of life came as I dug that well in my life. While my Prince worked in my garden, planting and rebuilding, I sat at His feet digging those wells of living water for myself and others.

Digging My Daughter's Well

The well I dug for my daughter started several years ago and it goes very deep. When she was young, we were very close. I was a single mom for four years of her life. When I married, we decided to raise our children in a loving Christian home. My husband adopted my daughter when she was seven, and she accepted the Lord when she was five years old. However, as she grew older, she became rebellious and made bad choices in her life.

It was very hard to watch her go through the things she chose for her life. All we could do was just be there for her in spite of how her husband treated us. She was still our daughter, and we loved her and tried very hard to love him.

Even though you raise your children to love the Lord, sometimes, they still rebel against you and the Lord. Not that we do what's wrong but it's the choices they make at the moment they open a door. My problem was I blamed myself for her rebellion. I punished myself and carried the guilt of it for a long time. It was not until several years later that the Lord began to teach me about generational curses and about not carrying their burdens of sins upon my back.

Those first years of her rebellion were very hard on me as a mother. Even though I knew the Lord, I still had Him under lock and key behind that wall I had built for Him. So many times in my frustration, my anger would rise up and we would have heated arguments.

When she met her ex-husband, (who is still unsaved), she was totally rebellious against the Lord, her dad, and me. This young man was and is still very disrespectful to our beliefs in the Lord and to us personally. He pulled her away from all she had been taught and tried to destroy our relationship and her belief in the Lord. When she got pregnant and moved out, peace finally returned to my home because all the rebellion had left.

Without even realizing it, one day, I started building a well for her. I was in a class where the teacher was breaking down the Word in Ezekiel 11:

19, which says that God will take the stony heart out, replace it with a heart of flesh, and give them a heart after God. I grabbed hold of that living water for her personally, and I began to dig that well of living water by praising and standing on the Word of God for her. Then I added Jeremiah 29: 11-13, which says, "He knows the thoughts and plans He has for us, thoughts and plans for a hope and a future." Every day I claimed it over her life until one day, He reached down and grabbed her out of the pit of hell and saved her soul. He filled her with the Holy Spirit and restored our relationship. He placed her on the road she was always supposed to be on.

My daughter became a well that I have had to continue to dig and pray over even to this day. Because I believe we are never done praying for each of the ones the Lord puts in our lives. As I dug that well, I began to discover all these generational curses that were in her and me. Every time the Lord showed me one, He led me to the waters of healing for both of us. Even when He leads us to healing waters, it is our choice to accept it or not.

As I have dug that well of prayer, praise, and healing for her, I have had to learn to run into my Prince's arms at times when I am hurt by certain issues that come up and I do not understand. We have continued to love and pray for our ex-son-in-law with the Lord's help.

I have watched my daughter struggle with many of the same issues I have had in my own life. For example, she continues to let people abuse her mentally and emotionally, no matter what it costs her. Her pain tolerance is very high in that area and she longs to be accepted and loved by people. Like me, she trusts the ones who use and abuse her. I keep praying she will wake up and stop letting people control who she is. I stand on the promise that the Lord will set her free, as I keep digging those wells of truth for her.

One of the hardest things for me is when I know the Lord is speaking to me about her, and I have to be still and sit back letting her bump into that wall over and over again or go around the mountain repeatedly. Somehow, she forgets I have been around those mountains so many times. Believe me, I have learned from my mistakes!

There have been times when she runs to everyone else but the Lord for advice, seeking man's approval. It hurts so much inside because I want her to grab hold of the truth that I want her to be free just like I want all of God's children to be free from bondage. At these times, I know I must dig deeper into those wells of prayer, praise, and freedom for her. I also know because I have learned that I must lean, trust, and rely upon my Prince even more because He is the only one who can totally set her free.

She met her current husband when they were kids at church. He was her first boyfriend. I pray their marriage will be successful. It is not perfect because no marriage is ever perfect but I see God working. As long as they trust God to build their marriage, they will make it.

I believe the Lord taught me how to dig those wells of prayer so I could teach others how to do the same. My daughter and I are very close. We still have days when we disagree but we have learned how to pray through them. She is a good mom and she is learning how to dig her own wells for her children. We have also learned how not to allow other people to come between us. The Enemy loves nothing better than to divide families. I have prayed very hard for our family to stay close and God has been faithful to answer that prayer for me.

Digging Wells for My Three Sons

I also have dug wells for my three sons who accepted the Lord at very young ages but in their teen years turned away from Him. Many days, I would sit in my quiet place weeping over them because again, I felt guilty. It was so hard to watch them struggle over their salvation.

Our Oldest Son

Our oldest son is a gift from the Lord. I was not supposed to have any more children after I lost a baby. I cried and prayed for the Lord to allow me to have more children. A year after my miscarriage, God blessed us with our son.

There are seven years between his sister and him. He loved to read the Bible and would bring it to me every day asking me to read his favorite story, "Dry Bones." The Lord showed me years later that every time my son brought the Bible to me as a child to read that story the Lord used it to bring life to my spirit.

He was very tall and skinny and at age three, he still walked with his feet turned in. At a Bible study, God spoke through a prayer that He was going to heal him, and he would be a preacher and evangelist. He was healed that day and walked straight from that day on.

It was as if that spark lit something in him. He loved Jesus so much and he understood beyond his years the salvation message. He was saved at five and baptized at seven. God had set his hand upon him but he would walk through many trials on the way. He kept himself before the Lord though and was able to attend an internship where he met his wife. He has been rejected by the church many times and he still struggles with that. I have had to sit back and watch him fight with so many things.

When he was about sixteen, he was late getting home one night, and I was walking the floor worried. The Lord spoke very clearly to me and asked me if I trusted Him. I said, "Of course, I do, but I am worried." The Lord said, "Do you not realize I love him even more than you ever will?" With that I said, "Lord, I am sorry and I will trust You from now on." I went back to bed, and in a few minutes he walked in.

Our son is married now and has three sons and a daughter. The oldest is named after the book in the Bible where his Daddy's favorite story is from. I watched him as he honored the Lord and saved himself for his wife. When they married it was as if they had kissed for the first time.

He tried to step out on his own to run after the promises of God but it was not the time yet. We all have to go through situations to become who God has called us to be. He struggles with his walk at times but I continue to stand on the promises that we were given before he was born. We trained him to love the Lord and serve Him with all his heart. I know God will never forget the calling He has put on our son's life, and the Lord will fulfil it to the fullness. I pray for our son daily that he will be the husband and father God called him to be and also that he will learn to walk in the courts of the Lord. Those wells of the Word run very deep for him and his little family. I believe the Lord will have our son fulfill all He has called him to do. I continue to pray for him to surrender all to the Lord and walk out everything God has for him.

Our Middle Son

Our middle son was also a miracle baby. He was born two and a half years after his brother, and it was also a battle to carry him from day one. God had His hand upon him and me. This child never sat still from the time he crawled. He was always busy! He followed after his brother and came to the Lord at a young age. He was saved at six and baptized at nine. He always believed in the impossible.

One day, in early October when he was nine years old, he really wanted it to snow. I explained that it was too soon. He said, "I will pray then and ask God to let it snow." The next day we awoke to several inches on the ground and tree limbs broken. It was one of the biggest snow storms in the history of our state. They still talk about it every year on the news. This built his faith so much.

He also loved to sing and worship the Lord. He had a gift of hearing music on an instrument. He walked with the Lord until he was about sixteen years old. Then he decided that his friends and the world looked better so he traveled on a road that was away from the Lord for several years. During that time, I just had to be still and allow him to walk on that road he had chosen.

It was very hard as a mom to watch my kids go through all this, but I knew what the Lord had said about them. Many times I did voice my opinion about what they were doing. It usually ended up in a battle, so I learned to run to the Lord and cry out for them. I prayed the Word constantly over them that God would set them free.

He was always with a girl who would use him and say she loved him but really it was all about what she could get from him. When he finally came back to the Lord the first time, he was without a job and was having trouble holding one. Fear had gripped him, and he could not follow through.

After feeling like he was never going to meet the right girl and praying constantly about it, one day he thought he did. For two years, she became part of our family. He was walking in the world but trying to walk with God too. I saw some of it but I turned a blind eye because I realized he really loved her. Then the bottom fell out of his life after she left him saying the spark had gone out months before. My son fell on his face at that point and cried out to the Lord. He gave his life back to the Lord and began a walk that truly has been a roller coaster ride.

God has been faithful to him and has walked him through all the challenges he has faced. I have watched him fast, pray and cry over her for days. He finally came to the point where he had to give her over to the Lord and trust Him for her soul. He gave away everything that she ever gave him and burned all her pictures. This was his way of letting her go. I have watched him as he has drawn closer to the Lord be able to truly forgive her for all that happened.

He is waiting upon the Lord now to bring his soul mate to him. He wants a woman who will love and respect him, not use him. He says he wants everything God wants for him. God is teaching him how to wait and trust Him each day. His faith is growing and the song God put in his heart as a child is coming back. He still believes in the God who can even answer a child's prayer for snow in October.

The gift of song and music is coming back as well as all the Lord placed in his heart to do. He believes he is called by the Lord. I can see that happening as he continues on the road God has called him to walk on. It is true if you train your children to love the Lord, they may stray for a time but God is always faithful to call them back to Him. I believe he will lead many to the Lord because the Lord has said it repeatedly to him through others. He is in training right now but soon there is a day coming when he will step into the place God has called him to. He will be bold and fearless for the Lord.

Our Youngest Son

Our youngest son was also a gift from the Lord. He was born nineteen months after his brother. He too loved Jesus and walked after Him when he was young. He was saved at five and baptized when he was eight. He always followed after his brothers so he also fell into the things of the world. He was always the one to make me smile even when I was having a tough day.

At age fifteen, my brother and sister-in-law offered to take him for a school year. They lived across the country. We agreed because we wanted better for him. Then all the negative talk began because they could supply him with all he needed and even wanted. We did not have that ability. They acted like we did not teach our children anything and we had been awful parents. They decided they were going to take our parental rights away so they could get money from us to help support him. We had to have them send him home before the school year was done. They gave him a round trip ticket so he could leave us if he chose to. I knew in my heart that we had to stand our ground. Our son chose to stay with his family. I am so thankful the Lord answered our prayers. My brother and sister in law were angry with us for the choice we had made. He said to me that love does not put clothes on our kid's backs or shoes on their feet. Well that's what our family was and always will be based on – love. I believe that faith, hope, and love should be the foundation of every family.

All the words hurt so much. I had to take them before the Lord and forgive them for all that was said and done, I love my brother and my sister in law. I know now that they were doing what they thought was right, but God gave us our son to raise and no matter how hard things were he should have never of gone to live there, A visit should have been enough.

It took years for our son to forgive us for making him come home. He liked the rich life they lived but it gave him this attitude that he was entitled to us taking care of him. He thought we were to support him and do everything for him. He kept himself in the world and refused to help his dad with anything. Sometimes, he mocked what we had taught him. We allowed him to stay with us at times because he is our son and because we believe in the Word of God. It says that your ministry starts in your home.

I always felt that because I was called to minister, I could never turn my own children away. How could I go out and minister to others if I could not help my own children? I believe that because we have shown him love, he still wants to be around his family.

As he has gotten older, he finally understands why we brought him home. He continues every year to honor us more and more as his parents and this blesses my heart. I also believe it is what will bring him back to the Lord. Because the roots run very deep in him and the promise is there; he will open his eyes and see the truth. I believe he knows the truth already. God has reassured me that He has His hand upon him, and He will never let him go. I also believe that as he watches his brothers and sister follow the Lord, he will follow after them.

Wells for Our Grandchildren

Years ago, I started digging wells for each grandchild God has blessed us with. We have eleven grandchildren right now but I know there are many more little blessings to come. Not all of them are serving Him but I know my prayers are being heard and as I speak the Word over them, the Lord will honor it.

Letting Go

While I dug those living wells of prayer, praise, and the Word over my children, it was in those moments that I finally realized I had to let them go too. I had to trust my Prince to bring them back. One day, while I sat in my garden weeping, He told me it was time for me to know that His promises are true. He then said that He loved my children more than I could ever love them. I had to believe that because we raised them up to love the Lord, they will return to Him. In other words, take Him at His Word and His promise.

I have had to stand on that word over and over again. As I have let them bump their heads against the wall, I have watched as three of them have returned to the love and service of the Lord. The Word is true and I know in my heart that, as I continue to dig that well for the other one, God will be faithful to His Word. He will also return to those roots that were planted in his heart from the beginning.

It has been a walk of learning to trust Him and giving them to Him every day. It is digging those wells of prayer, praise, and the Word over them knowing that His Word never returns to Him void. It always accomplishes the purpose and plan it was set out to do.

Life is full of bumps in the road but it is how we choose to treat those bumps that counts. Do we run to the King seeking His wisdom or do we try to figure it out for ourselves? For too many years, I stayed in bondage of trying to figure it out for myself. I was lazy about my walk with my King. I wanted all the benefits of being called a King's kid but I did not want to do anything to build that relationship.

Wells of Prayers, Praise, and the Word

A time comes in all our lives where we must trust God and grow up in Him. We must know without a doubt that if we have accepted Him to be the keeper of our heart's garden that He has our best interest at heart. We must learn to stand on His promises and not be moved to the left or to the right. Sometimes, growing up hurts but for the most part, it is an amazing thing to look back and see His loving hands upon our lives.

We have to stand on the Word and the truth, and we must dig those wells so that we will be free to stand. When we are free, we can help set others free. I have dug many wells of prayer, praise and the Word for many people the Lord has given me. I am so thankful for the time I have spent digging those wells. I am also thankful for the ones in the future that He will give me to dig. I have learned so much in the time I have spent being obedient to Him.

Today more than ever before I believe in all our lives we need to be digging those wells of prayer, praise and the Word, not only for our families but also for the ones the King of Kings puts in our paths. When we dig the wells, He pours the water of the living Word upon their lives and it heals and changes them. Test Him and take Him at His word because He is faithful to all His promises.

All things work together for the good of those who love Him. Digging those wells of praise, prayer, and the Word always work together for the good of those who love Him.

Today, I can look around my heart's garden and know I have wells of living water running strong in it. I still have wells to dig for new people He puts in my path, and I still continue to dig out deeper ones for the people in my life. My Prince has taught me so much about the depth of His Word, and I am very thankful as He takes me in His loving arms. I know now I can whisper in His ear, "I love you," and He will respond with, "I love you even more."

As He takes my hand in His and I look into those beautiful piercing eyes, my heart floods with peace and joy. We quietly walk together in that peace and harmony, and He says to me, "Dance with Me, My love." As He embraces me in His arms and we begin to waltz, my heart is overjoyed for the love that I am surrounded with now.

Chapter 13

WALTZING IN HIS COURTS

Again, I stood in that beautiful garden on a day when the Lord was getting ready to so lovingly instruct me. The work of healing that had taken place in my heart was truly a work of art.

As I stood in the midst of my garden I could feel the breeze in my hair, and there was a longing in my heart to see my Prince of Peace. Suddenly, I heard His steps coming in the distance. My heart began to pound loudly at the thought of seeing my Prince again.

As He came into view, I ran into His loving arms, excited to see Him again. He embraced me and whispered in my ear that He loves me. Then He took my hand in His and said, "Walk with Me for a while." As we walked slowly through my garden, He began to talk to me about my life as a worshiper. He told me how much He loves it when I worship Him. Then He said that there were more things that I needed to learn about being a worshiper.

He spent a lot of time and care rebuilding and replanting my heart's garden. He had done a great work there, and I was truly thankful for all that had been accomplished. However, the area of worship had not been touched. I was always a worshiper but I was immature in my worship. I did not know or understand this until the day my Prince of Peace showed me the truth about my worship.

I always thought worship was when you came together with others, sang songs, closed your eyes and loved Him. I always tried to stand and just bask in His presence but the thoughts of the past and the unworthiness of who I was would keep me from truly entering into His presence and into His worship.

On the day that my Prince and I took that walk, He showed me what I had been doing in worship. The truth He revealed caused me to fall on my face at His feet and asked Him to forgive me. As He took my hands in His and helped me to my feet again, He embraced me in His arms of love and whispered in my ear that I was forgiven. He told me I was loved with an everlasting love. He then began to share with me things about worship that I had never understood before.

Over the years, I was a little broken vessel, crying and pleading with Him as I worshiped, instead of loving Him. I had always seen myself as a broken vessel, unworthy to enter into the Holy of Holies. Even though He had healed me, this area still suffered. I felt so much shame and unworthiness to even be in the presence of the King that every time I entered the Holy of Holies during worship, I would hold my head down.

I lived according to my outward circumstances. If things were going good, I was happy. If things were going bad, I felt sad. I carried all these problems into worship with me when I should have left them at the door.

The shame and unworthiness were the worst parts because I always felt that I could never be forgiven because of what had happened to me. I thought I had done so many things wrong. I figured God could forgive me of my personal sins but I had no assurance He could take away the shame I felt. All those years, I carried the burden of believing I was at fault for the terrible things my stepfather did to me.

To me, everyone else was pure and clean. I would look around at all the people and see some enter into the Holy of Holies. I thought, "Well, they must have never done anything as bad as me, so the Lord lets them come in."

It was a battle to get past those outer courts, where I ran around crying and weeping over the past failures. I constantly shared my woes with the people who were stuck in the outer courts of bondage with me.

Fear of the unknown would always take hold of me. Even though I could look into the Holy of Holies and all I needed to do was walk forward, the thought of laying down all the junk was holding me captive.

On those days, even though I had worshiped, I left feeling empty and dry inside. Sometimes, when I completely got self out of the picture, I could go into the Holy of Holies.

I needed the Lord to renew my mind. The Lord had to bring balance to my life. He had to teach me that no matter what my circumstances, He is worthy to be worshiped.

Finally, God broke the chains of shame and freedom came. My spiritual eyes were opened. I saw that my Prince of Peace is always waiting for me to come and worship Him. He showed me I did nothing wrong to make my stepfather do the things

He did to me. He taught me with His love that I cannot carry that shame of the past because I was a little girl. It was never my choice to do the things that my stepfather made me do. I no longer feel like I have to stand at the door peering in. Now I can boldly enter His throne room, the Holy of Holies, because I am forgiven, washed in the blood of the Lamb with clean hands and a pure heart.

My Prince of Peace taught me about His love and worship. Today, I know that worship is not about us, our thoughts or our circumstances. It is about Jesus Christ. We must always be prepared to step into worship because He dwells with us. His presence is always with us.

 We cannot just walk in off the street and say, "Here I am to worship." Worship is every minute of every day. I can close my eyes at any moment of any day, just say His name, and I am in His presence in the Holy of Holies, standing before Him and loving Him. As I bask in His presence He embraces me in His loving arms and whispers in my ear, "Dance with me My love. "As we waltz together, joy floods my soul, for I know that I have found true worship..

No longer do I have to run and hide back in those familiar courts of doubt, fear, and unbelief, now there is joy in my worship. No longer do I worship out of my circumstances. It does not matter what is going on around me; my King is worthy to be worshiped. I no longer stand out in the outer courts playing games of the world. I know now that worship is not a performance or an act. It is a surrendering of our will to His will. His precious Holy Spirit longs to teach us if we will just get out of ourselves and allow Him to do it.

Transformation has taken place in my worship. I was like this little caterpillar stuck in her cocoon, not knowing what to do next. After my Prince stepped into my garden and removed the clouds of confusion, then the caterpillar kicked her way out of the cocoon and became a beautiful butterfly soaring along.

He loved me enough to teach me the truth about what worship is and I am very thankful. Worship is a true longing to know Him more. In my heart, I am desperate to know Him more every day. This is what worship is, when we come to that point in our lives where nothing else matters but spending time with Him. The things of this world no longer capture our attention. We finally understand how the psalmist felt when he said, "As the deer pants for water, so my soul thirsts for you." He truly does long for each of us to have a real relationship with Him so we can understand what real worship is. One of those things that must be right is our worship. We cannot worship Him right if we are held in the bondage to our the past.

Now as I step into His courts, I run into the Holy of Holies, because I am always ready to be with my Prince of Peace. Time stands still for me at those moments, and at times I never want to leave.

I run into His arms and we embrace again. He whispers in my ear, "Dance with me my love." We begin to waltz, and my eyes flood with tears of joy for all He has done for me. He kisses my cheek and tells me how much He loves me. He embraces me as we waltz throughout my garden. I know in my heart I will be able to come and worship my Prince of peace for all eternity.

Chapter 14

WALKING IN THE PALACE COURTS

The journey so far had been very long and hard, but as I look back on it I realize that it has been worth everything to reach this place where I stand today. The days of sitting at my King's feet and learning how to love others as He does have been rewarding. Now, when I stand in the midst of my garden, I am reminded of His great love for me. He took His love and poured it out upon my heart and healed all the wounds that had been there. He healed me so completely that now it is my time to walk in the destiny He has called me to.

As I stood in my garden once again I looked around, and all I could see was the beauty of what he had done for me. My heart flooded with love for Him. I longed for my Prince to come and talk with me. Suddenly, in the distance I heard those beautiful footsteps coming towards me. As I turned, I saw my Prince walking slowly through the flowers. I began to walk towards Him and as we met, He embraced me. I felt the warmth of His presence and His love flooded my heart once again.

He gently kissed my forehead and looked me in the eyes and said, "It's time for you to come to My palace and walk in My courts. "He said that this time, there had all been completed and that it had been a time of healing and learning. It also was a time of preparing me to walk in His palace courts. He asked me if I was willing to go with Him. I knelt down crying at his feet, kissed them, and said, "Yes, I will go." I felt so humbled that He would want me to go to His palace. He took my hands and helped me to my feet, and we began to walk toward the horizon.

As we continued to walk, I saw a beautiful palace sitting upon a hill. It was surrounded by my garden of flowers and trees. Everywhere I looked, I saw beauty. The palace was beautiful to behold. The sun shone down on it and made it look like gold. As we approached the palace, I saw huge angels standing there lined up on both sides of the walkway. They were singing, "Hallelujah" to the King. As we walked through that walkway up to the palace doors, He kept my hand in His. The doors opened, and we walked through a beautiful entryway. There were lovely tapestries all over the walls and gold was everywhere. My heart was overwhelmed with love for my King.

As we stood in the middle of that great entryway He took my hands in His and said, "This is where you have always belonged. You will have some angels who will attend to you now." He kissed my forehead and whispered, "I love you" once again. I watched as He turned and walked out of that room.

I was taken to a room where I was prepared to walk in His courts. Anointing oil was poured over my head and down to my feet. The white dress I had been wearing for so long had now turned golden. It had layers of beautiful colors under that golden color. The dress was covered with splendid jewels and embroidery designs throughout. My hair was braided and had flowers woven in it. A crown of jewels was placed upon my head. Then I was led up a staircase. At the top of the staircase, hung a beautiful purple curtain. I waited for the curtain to open.

As I waited, it seemed like an eternity as they continued to prepare me to go into the presence of the King. They wanted everything to be perfect when the curtain opened. The gold bracelet on my right wrist with writing on it said, "Daughter of the Most High." The gold bracelet on my left wrist had my God-given name on it. It was as if all the things I had been dreaming of were finally coming true. I had known for many years that I was called to minister but I always seemed to be held back for some reason. I knew He wanted me to walk with power and authority. I knew I was called to speak healing into His people's lives.

I had always held myself back because I felt inferior to others and I was not trained as well as others. I knew the Lord wanted me to step into the purpose and plans that He has for me. Many days, I sensed I was walking in that place but then something would happen to make me feel so worthless. Consequently, I doubted God's calling on my life.

However, my Prince decided it was time to be my teacher and guide. He determined that no man would ever receive His glory. He knew my heart and that for years, I had looked for man's approval. In my mind, it was man who would help me move forward. Perhaps, some pastor would finally release me to do all that God called me to do. I always watched on the sidelines as pastors released others to go out and minister but they seemed blinded to what God called me to. That led to many days of discouragement because I thought if they could not see my ministry, I must have heard the Lord wrong. In my frustration, I would run looking for acceptance and for the gifts in me to be pushed forward.

It has been a long and tedious journey to this place. As a matter of fact, it was somewhat like being imprisoned just waiting for the Lord to release me to do His work. He had already done the healing in me but I was stuck for several years. In retrospect, I can see how the Lord was putting everything in place for me to step forward. For a few moments, God would use me but then all my gifts would seem to be stripped away from me.

I did not understand why this was happening to me but I made up my mind I was not going to give up. As weak as I felt in my heart and spirit at times, I held on because I knew what He had already done in my heart. I had to believe He brought me into His palace for kingdom purposes.

At this point, my walk became very lonely. The Lord pulled us away from our church, and we had no home church. We went to different churches but never found a place. The closest we came was a good friend's church. She saw God in me and the gifts that He had placed there. She was the only one at that point who believed in me and what God wanted to do in my life. She opened up her pulpit and allowed me to minister to God's people. For that I will forever be grateful to my sister and friend, Pastor Earline Jones of Amazing Grace Church. If not for her during those dry times and allowing me to step into those shoes, I might have just given up on the promise. I really thought that was where the Lord was going to plant us, but He had different plans for my life.

In August of 2016, the Lord opened a door again for me to attend another gathering at Esther's House in Butler, Mo. I had already been there twice and to be able to return was such a blessing. I entered 2016 not very good spiritually. I felt defeated and very alone. I knew the Lord was with me but still felt like I was never going to connect. On April 25th, I lost my momma, and I was really feeling low. I knew I needed a breakthrough out of the dark place I was in. One day, as I was telling a friend about Esther's House, she asked if I would ever go back. I said, "I don't think they will ever let me come back because I have been there two times already."

On Mother's Day, as I wished my friend Jai a happy day she said, "My Mom says that if you would like to come back to Esther's house for a gathering, the invitation was open to you." My spirit jumped inside me because I knew that the invitation from Dr. Joyce came because the Lord had spoken to her. I knew that the Lord had heard my prayer. I said, "Yes, I want to go."

I asked Jai to pray for me. I told her that all I wanted was to sit in the Lord's presence. I didn't care if I got a word or not; my only desire to sit in His presence so I could hear Him again. At that point in my life, it seemed as if the heavens were as brass to me. I felt like I was praying to a brick wall at times; yet, I knew I was standing there at that curtain waiting to be allowed into the courts. I knew it, but all seemed dark around me. I even feared that I would never be released from this prison of just waiting. My hands seemed to be tied up. I could not move to the left or right.

The day came for me to go to the gathering. As I got up that morning to prepare to go, the Lord said to me, "This is a new day and a new season for you." The prayer and cry of my heart was, "Lord, please just meet me there." As my son drove me, we talked a little but mostly I prayed in the spirit. As we got closer to the gathering, I began to weep because the Lord was not only going to meet me there, He was escorting me there. I wept at His presence. I felt loved and honored to be able to go back again.

When I walked in that place, the first thing Dr. Joyce said to me, "As you walked in and I saw your feet the Lord said "It's a new season for you Tammy" I knew immediately I had walked into a time of destiny for my life. During those three days, I was treated like a queen in the palace courts. The Lord ministered to me in such a great way. When the Word came, it healed deeply.

The Lord spoke about my perseverance and the

hiding place He had me in. He talked about the stripping of the coat of many colors — the gifts and talents He has placed in my heart. He talked about how He has set me apart for His kingdom and how he predestined me to walk with Him in the palace courts of heaven. He even spoke about how He had protected me from generational curses and how the Enemy tried to destroy me. He said He had me in this dark place so He could finish the piercing of my heart, the circumcision of my heart. Then I could stand before Him with pure hands and a clean heart.

He told me the gifts and talents had been stripped away, He was giving me new treasures and a mantle of authority to speak the truth into His people's lives. He released me out of that place of lockdown and opened the curtains so I could walk into newness of life. He always wanted me to hear Him in a deeper way.

I learned that day why the waiting had taken so long. As I surrendered it all to Him, joy filled my heart again and peace overwhelmed me. I realized that the journey to this point had begun way back in 2002 when I visited Esther's house for the first time. He had opened my heart at that point, and I let Him out of the prison wall of lattice I had him behind. The second time I went in 2012 was about me knowing that He was in charge of my upbringing in Him. He wanted me to know I am beautiful inside and out. I am beautiful in His eyes, and that is all that matters. This time was about His perfect completion.

One of the things He told me was that He was going to send me to a prepared place. In September of 2016, the Lord sent us to a church again where we finally feel at home. It's even more than that though; it's that I did not have to tell the Pastor I was a minister; God told him. So I know the Lord has all this. He has begun to open a door for me to minister, and I am believing the Lord will open up doors abundantly for me. It seems like all the doors I have tried to open in the past but failed are finally opening. It has been my heart's desire to do His will. I long to see His people filled, healed, and set free.

When the Lord took me to His palace to be prepared and released by Him. I had no idea it would take so very long. It was like He had settled it in my heart that no man was ever going to release me but Him. It took time, yes! I knew though that when my Prince was done preparing me, I would walk in the places that He had called me to. He lovingly and patiently took His time with me. As I waited in the outer courts to go into the throne room I learned how to walk as a princess. I learned that I was beautiful to Him. I even learned how to smile and laugh again. Though at times it seemed so lonely, I knew He was working on my heart and changing me. I so longed to go into that place on the other side of that curtain, but when I tried, the Lord would just say, "Not yet." I had to learn how to wait.

My garden became a place of learning and abiding in His presence. Resting in Him became my strength. When my heart was completely healed, it was time to walk in those palace courts. I knew no one could ever take that away from me. I knew that I had searched and found something in my King that very few find. I had finally moved past all those things and people I thought were holding me back. Now, I see who He called me to be all along. Finally I could see my true destiny. I am a daughter of His destiny.

There were many garments that had been given me, and each one meant something. They layered that golden dress that was put on me. These garments were praise, worship, trust, abiding, faith, hope, love, and forgiveness. Then I was given favor, power, boldness, authority, peace, and healing. Then garments from past generations were given to me because I was found worthy to carry those mantles. Each one was woven into those layers of that beautiful dress to remind me that I am to walk in the palace courts with the King. As I walked up each step to get to this point in my life, some steps were not easy to accept. Knowing you are called to walk in the palace courts of the King and getting there can be very difficult at times.

I had to learn how to die to self. Of course, this presented many challenges because we all want it our own way. Once I humbled myself to His will and not mine, it became much easier. Those steps of forgiveness, faith, hope, and love became easy after my Prince strengthened me to walk through the tough times. I think the hardest part for me was believing I was called to minister for the Lord.

It was years before any of the healing in my garden had even begun when He stepped into my life. As my husband and I sat on our couch one evening worshiping, we were suddenly caught up in the spirit. I found myself standing before the Lord crying. As I bowed before Him, He began to speak to me about what He was calling me to do for Him. I said, "Lord, I cannot do any of that because I am so unworthy."

He told me He had called me to minister to His people. He said I was called to speak into their lives so they could be filled, healed, and set free by His authority and power that lived in me. I kept telling Him, "Lord, I cannot because of this or that." But he insisted asking, "Will you do it for Me?" I kept avoiding the answer because of fear.

Finally, after He showed me several men and women who needed to hear the testimony of healing that He would do in my life, I said, "Yes, I will go for You Lord. I do not know how You will make that happen because I am a mess, Lord, but I will trust You." He said I would receive complete healing of my physical body, my spirit, and my emotions. He told me He was going to do such a great work in me that when it was complete, people would not even recognize me.

He also told me that He was going to give me power and authority to walk into places and take back what the Enemy had stolen from men and women of all backgrounds. The enemy will have to restore all he stole from me and my family. He asked me three times if I would go and preach the gospel, lay hands on the sick, and pray for them to be healed. I said, "Yes," every time He asked, but I depended on Him to tell me each time that I was worthy to walk in that realm of authority.

I remember saying, "Lord there are others much more qualified than me." He always said, "No one can fill the shoes I have called you to." He told me there were men and women just waiting on me to share my testimony with them. After battling with the call, I agreed to obey. I cried and cried because I just could not believe that He would call me to do anything. I came out of that time with Him to find out that while the Lord was speaking to me for those hours that I wrestled with Him, He was also speaking to my husband and telling him the same thing about me.

My husband said afterwards that it was an awesome experience. He told me what the Lord had told him and that he knew he would have to be very supportive of me. He truly has been my help and my sounding board many times. He is a very quiet man with lots of wisdom. He loves the Lord very much and he loves me. He has stood by me and helped me through the process of healing and loved me even when I could not love myself.

I also had to come to grips with the fact that it did not matter what anyone thought about me. All that mattered was what the Lord thought. Most people considered me a radical Christian and probably still do. I had to get to the point of not following the crowd because I wanted to be accepted. I had to stand upon what I believed and nothing else. At this point in my life, I really do not care what anyone thinks. I love the Lord with all my heart and no one will ever take that from me.

While healing was taking place in that garden, he was preparing me to walk in His palace courts. God wants this for all believers but I think that very few choose to walk on this road. Wide is the road that leads to destruction and narrow is the road that leads to Him. I chose the very narrow road and I am so thankful I did. I chose a long time ago to always seek more of Him in my life. I pray that for everyone He puts in my path because there is nothing like truly knowing Him.

As I waited behind that beautiful curtain for that moment when it would open for me, I thought about all the battles I had been through. I thought about the war that had raged in my heart and how it had almost been destroyed. I was overjoyed to know that finally, I would walk into the palace courts of the King. I knew what that meant! It was what He had talked about many years ago when He asked me if I was willing to go out for Him. I knew I would finally have direct access to my King any moment I needed Him. Not that I didn't already know, but just knowing that the calling and the release to go minister for Him was on the other side of that curtain was overwhelming to me.

The new beginning of the journey was getting ready to happen in my life and it was exciting to even think about it. I anticipated the new open doors. I was elated to know I was finally going to fulfill the calling and destiny He had prepared for me. I could barely take it all in. Doubts were removed. It was not me doing anything; it was all Him. I wanted to be in His perfect will. Finally, everything was done and I was ready to go before the King.

My heart pounded and as the curtain opened up slowly, my eyes caught the breath-taking beauty of the throne room. It had golden walls and beautiful tapestries on the floors. I looked ahead and my Prince caught my eyes. He was sitting on His throne dressed in gold and purple. As I stepped forward, He stood and stretched out His scepter, granting me entrance into His throne room. The crown on His head was beautiful. It spoke of His authority and presence. As I began to walk toward Him tears of joy trickled down my face. Time seemed to stand still as I walked that long carpeted aisle to Him. I touched the scepter he held out to me when I reached Him and then kneeled before Him. I laid my crown at His feet and cried for such great joy overtook me.

He took my hands in His and helped me to my feet. He picked up my crown and placed it back upon my head. Very lovingly, He wiped the tears from my eyes. Then He spoke to me, charging me with orders of walking in His palace as a daughter of the Most High should walk. He told me to carry the calling He had placed upon my life with that of a daughter of the Most High and gave me boldness and authority. He told me I had always been called to walk in the palace courts; it was always inside me but now, all the gifts and anointing were going to come forth. All I had to do was come before Him and ask; He will grant it to me because I am His daughter.

This was such a humbling thought because all I have ever wanted was to be used to help His people. I have always dreamed of going into His throne room and asking for whatever anyone needed. As I stood there crying, He said, "Only believe, all things are possible."

All things are possible with Him! All we have to do is believe. He took my face in His hands and reached forward, kissing my forehead. With my hands in His, He reached forward kissing them and said my hands were anointed with the healing of His hands. He then leaned forward and whispered in my ear, "My love, dance with me."

As we stepped out into this beautiful room and began to waltz, my heart flooded with joy. I knew I would never have to leave His arms again. I would walk in the palace courts forever. We danced to a love song from my heart to His and from His to mine. The music spoke of His great love for me and of my gratitude and love for Him. As we danced around that palace floor, joy overwhelmed my heart. I had come to rest in the arms of the Lover of my soul – at last. My Prince brought me to His palace where I could live as His daughter in His presence. I was finally home, and I knew I would never leave His side again.

Chapter 15

HEAVEN'S COMPLETION

Waltzing with God in the gardens of my heart has become such a great joy for me. I can now stand in the middle of my garden in the midst of those beautiful flowers. My white dress no longer has the rips, tears, and stains of my past on it. I now wear the beautiful dress of gold that carries the mantles of anointing. I finally know that I belong there in that garden of joy and peace with my Prince of Peace.

The journey has been long and hard. Many times I have wanted to quit pressing on but hope has continued to fill my heart's garden with love. Every ounce of my being bubbles over with joy for all He has done in my life. As I stand there in the midst of the gentle flowers of violet and blue with the sun bursting down on me, I am overwhelmed by the love I feel.

In the distance, I hear those wonderful footsteps again; those familiar steps I had heard in the past coming closer to me. I know it is my Prince of Peace coming to spend time with me. My heart pounds with the excitement of love for my King. He is coming to see me in my garden. As He approaches, my heart pounds faster until I can stand it no more. I run into His arms that await me with His love. As He embraces me in those loving arms, I feel the safety of a child in her Daddy's arms.

He embraces me, and He whispers in my ear, "Dance with Me, My love." As we begin to dance, it is as if we are floating through those fields of flowers. We stop, He kisses my forehead and tells me He loves me. Peace floods my soul, and I am overcome by His presence.

He takes my hand in His, and we begin to walk through my heart's gardens. As we walk, He begins to talk to me about all the things that have taken place in my garden. He reminds me of the walls, locks, and keys that I had placed on each wall I built. We return to each garden area. I look around now and all I can see is beauty.

The first area we persue is where I had him under lock and key behind that wall of lattice. He reminds me in a glimpse what it looked like before. I looked down in shame but He takes my face in His loving hands and lifts my head up; He looks me in the eyes. As His beautiful eyes once again pierce my soul I know He is lovingly showing me things of the past and how my heart looked. He reminds me that He did all that work in my garden for many reasons.

He broke me out of bondage, not only to free me but so He would have the freedom to heal all the broken areas in the garden of my heart. He is the garden keeper. It is up to us to let Him have access to every area of our hearts.

Time stood still in many of my garden areas because I was so broken and torn apart. My Prince of Peace stepped in every garden and healed each one completely. As I put myself in His loving arms and we waltzed in those gardens of hurt and pain, they became places of peace again. All the thorns and thistles began to be replaced with beautiful flowers of love. The more I placed my trust in Him, the more love flooded my heart.

As I learned to walk in those paths, more healing came. The more I ran into those arms of love, and the more we waltzed throughout those gardens, the more He taught me about myself and others. He has poured His great compassion and love into me, teaching me not only how to love and have compassion for others but also for myself. Each time I met with Him in the secret gardens of my heart, and we waltzed together, I grew stronger.

Many times I stand in the midst of those garden areas and sing the love songs of worship that flooded my heart to Him. I was so desperate to know Him and be with Him that it became the cry of my heart.

As I look around now I see nothing but hope. I know there will be more mountains to climb, but I also know He will climb them with me. He is the garden keeper and no mountain is too high for Him. Problems come and go, but it is how we face them that matters.

Again, I think about the Word that says, "Seek ye first the kingdom of God and His righteousness, and all these things will be added unto you." Righteousness means His way of thinking and doing things. I am finally seeking His way of doing things and that is what all of us must do in our lives. He is the keeper of our heart's garden; now all we must do is allow Him the opportunity to keep it.

I cannot allow any roots of bitterness, anger or offense to grow in my garden. toward any of those who have hurt me in the past or the ones who might hurt me in the future. I know I must run to my Prince of Peace and tell Him all my troubles and fears. Then He will wash them away with His love. In spite of all the pain He suffered on the cross, He continued to show His love and compassion for people, and I must do the same.

There is a price to be paid to have this peace and love fill our heart's gardens. The world will never understand why we do not want to run after its fleeting pleasures and have anger and hatred towards one another. The world responds to the people who hurt them with anger, hatred, and bitterness; they believe in revenge. However, we are called to respond in love. The world reacts to fear and offense. We are to trust in our God and turn our cheeks to the offense.

If we have truly allowed the Lord to complete the healing in our heart's gardens, we will walk with true love and compassion for others. Our hearts will be full of love, peace, and joy. Nothing in this world can compare with our relationship with the Prince of Peace.

Many people are searching for truth and walking around hurting. They search through the religious circles to find only emptiness. That is inevitable because religion will never give you peace. I know because I tried it.

I did the works and followed the rituals of man for years. I tried to find the Lord and peace through all the laws of religion. In the end, after looking in my heart, I found I still had my Prince of Peace locked up and barred from giving me what I searched for in futility.

I found out that His little portion of my heart's garden was a very small part, and that it was the only place where joy was found. Healing came to me, not through man or religion but through the Prince of Peace and a true relationship with Him.

Healing came because I was also willing to let Him access my garden of brokenness and pain and to uproot the things that had been planted there that were not right.

Healing and peace came as I allowed my Prince of Peace to plant new ideas of love and compassion into my heart and as He brought forth the truths of who I am in His eyes. He has completed a great work in my heart's gardens, and I am so thankful

In my life, I have great peace even though at times, my world looks pretty rough. I still know He is with me. As I stand in my garden in the midst of all His love, my heart is flooded with great joy. Beside me I feel His presence, my Prince of Peace. He takes my hand in His and turns to look at me. As I look in those beautiful eyes, I feel all the love He has for me, and I know I am His forever.

He leans forward, kisses me on my forehead, and embraces me with His loving arms. Then He whispers those wonderful words that my heart so longs to hear. "Dance with Me, My love." As we waltz together, I know I will be in His loving arms for eternity. We waltz together singing to each

other the love songs that have been completed in
the gardens of my heart.

Chapter 16

MINISTRIES & SCRIPTURES

THE MINISTRY OF STITCHES-N-LOVE
Reference - 1. Matthew 6: 33

As my journey progressed and healing began in my own life, God gave me a beautiful quilt ministry. It is full of His love and compassion for His people. Many hours of prayer have been put into this ministry. Without the Lord's direction, it would not even exist.

One morning as I was in prayer for a friend, I asked the Lord what I could possibly do for her other than pray. He reminded me of all the gifts He had placed in my hands. I loved to do hand work like embroidery. I continued to pray, and the Lord showed me a vision of a quilt for my friend. I drew it out on paper and then designed it on the material. That was in 2004. I took that quilt to her and the Lord blessed her with strength and peace.

From the moment the Lord showed me these quilts it blessed my life tremendously. With everyone He showed me I felt so humbled that He would trust me with such a task. Each one had a scripture written on it. I made the quilts, prayed over them, and asked the Lord what He would say to His people. I felt like it was Him guiding me. The scriptures came from His heart to theirs.

Many times, I battled inside about who the Lord wanted me to make it for. Amazingly, the persons who receive the quilts are always the ones God wants to have them. I never wanted to be doing things in myself, only to do God's will. Many people misjudged me, thinking I was making these quilts for attention. However judged I may have been, I know what God was doing in my heart.

With each one I made I became more confident in the Lord. I could actually see the healing that was taking place in my life and in the lives of others through the quilts. The designs were not mine; they were His — personally made for the receiver. God wanted to love His people, and I was a willing vessel.

After many quilts had been made and given from His heart, the Lord began to show me banners for the church. These banners represented what the Lord wanted to say to the body of Christ as a whole. Many people did not receive or understand why I made them. I was just being obedient to the Lord. I was putting on banners what He was telling me in my spirit for the body. They are very prophetic and have a message on them.

Many rejected them because they were not what they thought looked perfect. They are simple, yet, profound. I cried many times to the Lord because I felt the people were rejecting Him. I had to come to a place in my life where I had to just give this ministry back to the Lord. I feel when God's people are ready to receive His messages on the banners, He will have me bring them back into the church.

Sometimes, God's people do not want the truth staring them in the face. I had to let go of all the offense that I felt inside. The offense was not really against me but the Lord and what He was trying to tell His people. Healing came as I allowed the Lord to take the offense away. He told me to stop making banners because the church does not want to receive them. So I laid that ministry at the Lord's feet. I have given most of the banners away to the ones the Lord has led me to. The one I kept for my prayer room is a blessing to my family.

In 2007, my brother built me a website called stitchesnlove. I have connected with a few people who can see that the Lord gives us gifts to be used. Mine is a healing gift through quilts. He gives me a vision and I put it on fabric. I so long to see people healed and set free.

Most of the quilts I have made have been just given away because I felt like that is what God wanted me to do with them. I have prayed for provision to continue for many years. Although the Lord always provided for the quilt to be made, it has always been a sacrifice. The Lord has brought me to a point where this ministry is truly at His feet. I am no longer overflowing with the need to make them. That is probably because God has matured me in the prophetic. I believe one of the reasons I had to make the quilts was because I looked at myself as having no voice. I always thought, "How can I ever speak Lord? Who am I?"

After all this time, God was building up my faith in Him to believe that I can do all things through Him. He built up my confidence in Him by showing me visions of quilts and banners for His people. He taught me how to listen and obey. He taught me who I am in Him. He taught me that I do not have to fear man. He taught me to be bold and to take authority over the Enemy. He took a broken little girl and empowered her to be a bold and confident woman. All I care about is my God and what He thinks, not what man thinks. If I need anything He is right there.

I am not sure where this ministry is heading at this point in my life; all I know is I want the Lord's will for it. I am willing to do whatever He leads me to do. My prayer has always been to just give them away but there has to be provision for that if God wants it, so I leave it in His mighty hands. The website is out there but it has not been updated for a very long time.

I shared all this with you to say do not ever think what the Lord is telling you to do is silly. Remember, He uses the foolish things to confuse the wise. If He places something in your heart then do it to the best of your ability. Give Him glory and honor, and He will bless you for your obedience. Do not listen to man and his ways. Man will always reject God's ways. Even Christians sometimes reject what God wants to say and do. Just keep your eyes on Him and do what He tells you to do.

I pray that you will be encouraged to do all things for Christ to bring Him praise, honor, and glory.

THE QUILT

As I faced my Maker at the judgment, I knelt down before the Lord along with all the other souls. Before each of us laid our lives the squares of a quilt in many piles. An angel sat before each of us sewing our quilt squares together into a tapestry that is our life. But as my angel took each piece of cloth off the pile, I noticed how ragged and empty each of my squares was. They were filled with giant holes. Each square was labeled with a part of my life that had been difficult, the challenges and temptations I was faced with in everyday life. I saw hardships that I had endured, which were the largest holes of all.

I glanced around me. Nobody else had such squares. Other than a tiny hole here and there, the other tapestries were filled with rich colors and the bright hues of worldly fortune. I gazed upon my life and was disheartened. My angel was sewing the ragged pieces of cloth together threadbare and empty, like binding air. Finally, the time came when each life was to be displayed, held up to the light, the scrutiny of truth. The others rose; each in turn, holding up their tapestries. So filled their lives have been.

My angel looked upon me and nodded for me to rise. My gaze dropped to the ground in shame. I had not had all the earthly fortunes. I had love in my life and laughter. But there had also been many trials of illness, death, and false accusations that took my world as I knew it from me.

I had to start over many times. I often struggled with the temptation to quit, only to somehow master the strength to pick up and begin again. I spent many nights on my knees in prayer, asking for help and guidance in my life. I had often been held up to ridicule, which I endured painfully, each time offering it up to the father in hopes that I would not melt within my skin beneath the judgmental gaze of those who unfairly judged me. And now, I had to face the truth. My life was what it was, and I had to accept it for what it was. I rose slowly and lifted the combined squares of my life to the light: An awe filled gasp covered the air.

I gazed around at the others who stared at me with wide eyes. Then I looked upon the tapestry before me. Light flooded the many holes, creating an image, the face of Christ. Then our Lord stood before me with warmth and love in His eyes. He said, "Every time you gave over your life to me, it became My Life, My hardships and My struggles. Each point of light in your life is when you stepped aside and let Me shine through, until there was more of Me than there was of you."

My prayer is that all our quilts be threadbare and worn, allowing Christ to shine through.

Author Unknown

BECOMING DAUGHTERS OF DESTINY

Daughters of Destiny is another ministry the Lord placed in my hands in 2006. This ministry also has had a tough go of it. Many times, I tried to start it in a church only to feel rejected or to have it never go forward. The vision for this ministry is God-given. I have come to realize at this point in my own life that perhaps, the reason this ministry has not been launched the way I have always dreamed is that it may not be the time for it yet.

I have given it over to the Lord and when He opens the door for it to come forth, it will. However, in my times of waiting, He has continued to place women in my path who need healing in their lives. I continue to listen and obey Him to help them. I know He is the one guiding and leading me. I cannot do anything in myself. I know He is building women up to be a part of the ministry.

Early in this ministry, I found myself constantly frustrated because I desperately wanted to see God move and heal His people. I wanted Him to do it now. I did not want to wait or spend the time learning and growing. But He has taught me to be patient, to rest and be at peace in Him.

I am so grateful for the time He has spent teaching me. Now I wait for the King to say it's time. I know when He finally opens a door for me to go out and preach or share my testimony, it will be His doing. He has sent me out a few times to speak, and I have loved every moment of walking in the anointing. I long in my spirit to fulfil the destiny He has placed on my life. I long for Mark 16:15-18 Amplified to be established in my life

There is nothing that can compare to being in the Lord's will. As I said earlier, I pray for women all the time as the Lord leads them to me. If you need healing in your life, I am willing to pray with you. I know the Lord wants us all to be free. I am also available to speak. I pray you will find healing through my Prince so that you can walk in your destiny. May the Lord bless you beyond your expectations. *Numbers 6: 24-26 Amplified*

VISION FOR BECOMING THE
DAUGHTER'S OF DESTINY

For we are God's (own) handiwork. (His workmanship), recreated in Christ Jesus, (born anew) that we may do those good works which God predestined planned beforehand for us, (taking paths which He prepared ahead of time) that we should walk in them, (living the good life which He preordained and made ready for us to live) (Ephesians 2: 10, Amplified).

This is the vision the Lord has given me for Becoming Daughters of Destiny. The Lord wants all women to see and understand that He has preordained our lives to fulfill the destiny He has placed on each of us. The Lord's desire is for all women to be healed, filled, and set free in every area of our lives. He wants us to receive freedom so we can walk into the destiny He has called us to, so that the words of this scripture will be fulfilled.

How do we become free to walk into the destiny God has preordained for our lives?

1. We have to come to a point in our lives where we realize God does have a purpose

and a plan for us. We must not only believe it in our minds but in our hearts.

2. We must be willing to allow God to heal those wounds that are deep within our hearts. We must realize that there is nothing hidden from God.

3. As we seek the plan God has for us, we allow Him inside our hearts to heal the wounds that are there, and then we can see ourselves as God sees us.

4. As the revelation of God's love begins to shine the light of understanding, we step out in new founded faith. The walk becomes easier and strengthens us as we trust in the Lord. We must be teachable.

5. As freedom comes we are released to go forward to fulfill what God has called each of us to do.

Many women out there are just waiting for someone to speak a word into their lives so they can be free and move forward. They seem to be stuck in the past, in the bondage of depression, fear, anger, abandonment, rejection and many other things. The vision I have for Becoming Daughters of Destiny is to see women be free to come forward into what God has called them to do.

I want to teach them how to get hold of the Word and apply it to each situation in their lives. I want to teach them to lean, trust, rest and rely upon the Lord so that their walk with Him will be deepened. I want to teach them how to have freedom in worship and freedom to walk in the authority God has given each one of us.

I want to see Becoming Daughters of Destiny grow into a women's group that is in one accord and is reaching out to women who are hurting. Women are longing and searching for freedom, and they need to know that God does have a plan and purpose for them, that He does have something for them to do whether it is to pray, serve, or teach.

I want us all to know we are loved, and we are special. It is also very important as we learn to grow and be free that we reach out to others and encourage them to step out and be free also. Becoming Daughters of Destiny will reach each class of women whether they are young or old, black or white, rich or poor, it matters not.

The vision is to become well, to become one in the Lord. The vision is to give women hope. It is to set the captives free from bondage that has tormented their lives. The vision is to put the Enemy under our feet and take back the ground he has stolen from each of us.

Prayer is an important part of this vision because it helps us to hear the voice of God. We must lock arms in the spirit of agreement as we accept each other's burdens and go through the process of growth for our health, wealth, hopes and dreams for the future of our mission fields in our homes, churches, and communities.

As we move in one accord, we desire the Spirit to empower women to stand in their calling, grow in wisdom, truth, and discernment as they blossom into Becoming Daughters of Destiny.

God has called me to usher in the anointing, to release change and purpose in the lives of women and as the windows of heaven open His glory will fall. Walls will break down, strongholds will be destroyed. They will be enlightened of their real identities in Christ being established, and we will reach our destinies as true Daughters of the Most High Living God!

CONTACT TAMARA GUNN

Email: praiseandvictory@aol.com

Email: beadaughterofdestiny@g-mail.com

SCRIPTURES THAT HAVE
CHANGED MY LIFE

The Word of God has always been my life source. I have learned through the years to hide it in my heart. I am so thankful that my spiritual momma taught me the value of the Word and how to apply it to my life. I believe the whole Bible is our source of life. If we will take it in our hearts and apply it to our lives then it will change us. If we only read it and never take it in and apply it to our lives, it just becomes words. These scriptures have touched my life immensely, and I pray they will touch yours also.

For I know the thoughts and plans that I have for you, says the Lord, thoughts and plans for welfare and peace and not for evil, to give you hope in your final outcome. Then you will call upon Me, and you will come and pray to Me, and I will hear and heed you. Then you will seek Me, inquire for, and require Me (as a vital necessity) and find Me when you search for Me with all your heart (Jeremiah 29: 11-13, Amplified).

For we are God's (own) handiwork (His workmanship), recreated in Christ Jesus, (born anew) that we may do those good works which God predestined (planned beforehand) for us (taking paths which He prepared ahead of time) that we should walk in them (living the good life which he prearranged and made ready for us to live) (Ephesians 2: 10, Amplified).

We are assured and know that (God being a partner in their labor) all things work together and are (fitting into a plan) for good to and for those who love God and are called according to (His) design and purpose (Romans 8:28, Amplified).

But seek (aim at and strive after) first of all His kingdom and His righteousness (His way of doing and being right) and then all these things taken together will be given you besides (Matthew 6:33, Amplified).

You will guard him and keep him in perfect and constant peace whose mind (both its inclination and its character) is stayed on You, because he commits himself to You, leans on You, and hopes confidently in You. So trust in the Lord commit yourself to Him, lean on Him, hope confidently in Him forever; for the Lord God is an everlasting

(Rock the Rock of ages) (Isaiah 26: 3-4, Amplified).

The Lord is my Shepherd (to feed, guide, and shield me), I shall not lack. He makes me lie down in (fresh tender) green pastures; He leads me beside the still and restful waters. He refreshes and restores my life (my self); he leads me in the paths of righteousness (uprightness and right standing with Him not for my earning it, but) for His name's sake. Yes, though I walk through the (deep, sunless) valley of the shadow of death, I will fear or dread no evil, for You are with me; Your rod (to protect) and Your staff (to guide), they comfort me. You prepare a table before me in the presence of my enemies. You anoint my head with oil; my (brimming) cup runs over. Surely or only goodness, mercy, and unfailing love shall follow me all the days of my life, and through the length of my days the house of the Lord (and His presence) shall be my dwelling place (Psalm 23, Amplified).

The Lord bless you and watch, guard, and keep you; The Lord make His face to shine upon and enlighten you and be gracious (kind, merciful, and giving favor) to you; The Lord lift up His (approving) countenance upon you and give you peace (tranquility of heart and life continually) (Numbers 6:24-26, Amplified).

Although my father and my mother have forsaken me, yet the Lord will take me up (adopt me as His child) (Psalms 27:10, Amplified).

He who dwells in the secret place of the Most High shall remain stable and fixed under the shadow of the Almighty. (Whose power no foe can withstand). I will say of the Lord He is my Refuge and my Fortress, my God, on Him I lean and rely, and in Him I confidently trust! (Psalms 91:1-2, Amplified).

For he will give His angels especial charge over you to accompany and defend and preserve you in all your ways of obedience and service (Psalms 91:11, Amplified).

I will bless the Lord at all times; His praise shall continually be in my mouth. My life makes its boast in the Lord; let the humble and afflicted hear and be glad. O magnify the Lord with me, and let us exalt His name together. I sought (inquired of) the Lord and required Him (of necessity and on the authority of His word), and He heard me, and delivered me from all my fears (Psalms 34:1-4, Amplified).

The Lord will perfect that which concerns me. Your mercy and loving kindness, O Lord, endure forever-forsake not the works of Your own hands (Psalms 138:8, Amplified).

My frame was not hidden from You when I was being formed in secret (and) intricately and curiously wrought (as if embroidered with various colors) in the depths of the earth (a region of darkness and mystery). Your eyes saw my unformed substance and in Your book all the days (of my life) were written before ever they took shape, when as yet there was none of them. How precious and weighty also are Your thoughts to me. O God! How vast is the sum of them! If I could count them, they would be more in number than the sand. When I awoke, (could I count to the end) I would still be with You (Psalms 139:15-18, Amplified).

Lean on, trust in, and be confident in the Lord with all your heart and mind and do not rely on your own insight or understanding. In all your ways know recognize, and acknowledge Him, and He will direct and make straight and plain your paths. Be not wise in your own eyes; reverently fear and worship the Lord and turn (entirely) away from evil. It shall be health to your nerves and sinews and marrow and moistening to your bones (Proverbs 3:5-8, Amplified).

Keep and guard your heart with all vigilance and above all that you guard, for out of it flow springs of life (Proverbs 4:23, Amplified).

Death and life are in the power of the tongue, and they who indulge in it shall eat the fruit of it (for death or life) (Proverbs 18:21, Amplified).

But those who wait for the Lord (who expect, look for, and hope in Him) shall change and renew their strength and power they shall lift their wings and mount up (close to God) as eagles (mount up to the sun); they shall run and not be weary, they shall walk and not faint or become tired (Isaiah 40; 31, Amplified).

But He was wounded for our transgressions, He was bruised for our guilt and iniquities: the chastisement (needful to obtain) peace and well-being for us was upon Him, and with the stripes that wounded) Him we are healed and made whole (Isaiah 53:5, Amplified).

The Lord God is my Strength, my personal bravery, and my invincible army; He makes my feet like hinds feet and will make me to walk (not to stand still, but to walk) and make (spiritual) progress upon my high places (of trouble, suffering, or responsibility)! (Habakkuk 3:19, Amplified).

Have not I commanded you? Be strong, vigorous, and very courageous. Be not afraid, neither be dismayed, for the Lord your God is with you wherever you go (Joshua 1:9, Amplified).

A man's mind plans his way, but the Lord directs his steps and makes them sure (Proverbs 16:9, Amplified).

But Jesus looked at them and said. With men this is impossible, but all things are possible with God (Matthew 19:26, Amplified).

Pray, therefore, like this: Our father who is in heaven, hallowed (kept holy) be Your name. Your kingdom come, Your will be done on earth as it is in heaven. Give us this day our daily bread. And forgive us our debts, as we also have forgiven (left, remitted, and let go of our debts, and have given up resentment against) our debtors. And lead (bring us not into temptation, but deliver us from the evil one. For Yours is the kingdom and the power and the glory forever (Matthew 6:9-13, Amplified).

If you really love Me, you will keep (obey) My commands (John 15:13, Amplified).

If you live in Me (abide vitally united to Me) and My words remain in you and continue to live in your hearts, ask whatever you will, and it shall be done for you (John 15:7, Amplified).

Therefore, (there is) now no condemnation (no adjudging guilty of wrong) for those who are in Christ Jesus, who live (and) walk not after the dictates of the flesh, but after the dictates of the Spirit (Romans 8:1, Amplified).

For in (this) hope we were saved. But hope (the object of) which is seen is not hope. For how can one hope for what he already sees? But if we hope for what is still unseen by us, we wait for it with patience and composure (Romans 8:24-25, Amplified).

For I am persuaded beyond doubt (am sure) that neither death nor life, nor angels nor principalities, nor things to come, nor powers, nor height, nor depth, nor anything else in all creation will be able to separate us from the love of God which is in Christ Jesus our Lord (Romans 8:38-39, Amplified).

I have strength for all things in Christ! Who empowers me. (I am ready for anything and equal to anything through Him who infuses inner strength into me; I am self-sufficient in Christ's sufficiency (Philippians 4:13, Amplified).

MY FAMILY & PHOTO GALLERY

MY FAMILY

Family is very important to me. I have always tried to instill the love of the Lord and love of family in my children. We have are disagreements but we have learned to always forgive. I believe that the Lord taught me how to forgive and love unconditionally so that I could live it daily teaching my children and grandchildren how to live that way also. I pray every day to be able to teach this to others because it is what has brought me through all the things that happened in my life. I pray you will receive these scriptures in to your heart and ponder them. They are what my family is built upon. They will help you on your most difficult days as they have helped me. I pray you also will enjoy seeing the pictures of the ones that I love. God Bless!

1 Corinthians 13:4-13 Amplified

Love endures long and is patient and kind; love never is envious nor, boils over with jealousy, is not boastful or vainglorious, does not display itself haughtily. It is not conceited (arrogant and inflated with pride) it is not rude (unmannerly) and does not act unbecomingly. Love (God's love in us) does not insist on its own rights or its own way, for it is not self-seeking; it is not touchy or fretful or resentful; it takes no account of the evil done to it (it pays no attention to a suffered wrong). It does not rejoice at injustice and unrighteousness, but rejoices when right and truth prevail. Love bears up under anything and everything that comes, is ever ready to believe the best of every person, its hopes are fadeless under all circumstances, and it endures everything (without weakening). Love never fails (never fades out or becomes obsolete or comes to an end). As for prophecy (the gift of interpreting the divine will and purpose), it will be fulfilled and pass away; as for tongues, they will be destroyed and cease; as for knowledge, it will pass away (it will lose its value and be superseded by truth). For our knowledge is fragmentary (incomplete and imperfect), and our prophecy (our teaching) is fragmentary (incomplete and imperfect). But when the complete and perfect (total) comes, the incomplete and imperfect will vanish away (become antiquated, void, and superseded). When I was a child, I talked like a child, I thought like a child, I reasoned like a child; now that I have become a man, I am done with childish ways and have put them aside. For now we are looking in a mirror that gives only a dim (blurred) reflection (of reality as in a riddle or enigma), but then (when perfection comes) we shall see in reality and face to face! Now I know in part (imperfectly). But then I shall know and understand fully and clearly, even in the same manner as I have been fully and clearly known and understood (by God). And so faith, hope, love abide (faith conviction and belief respecting man's relation to God and divine things; hope joyful and confident expectation of eternal salvation; love true affection for God and man, growing out of God's love for and in us), these three; but the greatest of these is love.

Colossians 3:12-17 Amplified

Clothe yourselves therefore, as God's own chosen ones (His own picked representatives), (who are) purified and holy and well-beloved (by God Himself, by putting on behavior marked by) tenderhearted pity and mercy, kind feeling, a lowly opinion of yourselves, gentle ways, (and) patience (which is tireless and long-suffering, and has the power to endure whatever comes, with good temper). Be gentle and forbearing with one another and if, one has a difference (a grievance or complaint) against another, readily pardoning each other; even as the Lord has (freely forgiven you, so must you also (forgive). And above all these (put on) love and enfold yourselves with the bond of perfectness (which binds everything together completely in ideal harmony). And let the peace (soul harmony which comes) from Christ rule (act as umpire continually) in your hearts (deciding and settling with finality all questions that arise in your minds, in that peaceful state) to which as (members of Christ's) one body you were also called (to live). And be thankful (appreciative), (giving praise to God always). Let the word (spoken by) Christ (the Messiah) have its home (in your hearts and minds) and dwell in you in (all its) richness, as you teach and admonish and train one another in all insight and intelligence and wisdom (in spiritual things, and as you sing) psalms and hymns and spiritual songs, making melody to God with (His) grace in your hearts. And whatever you do (no matter what it is) in word or deed, do everything in the name of the Lord Jesus and in (dependence upon) His Person, giving praise to God the Father through Him.

Our Children Together, Nathan, Jacob, Matthew & Shana

Our daughter, Shana & her husband, George

Our oldest son, Nathan & his wife, Gloria

Our son, Jake & Our son;   Matthew and his girlfriend, Mikaela

Mother Daughter Tea
2017

All my girls and
one little guy.

Christmas 2017

Our sons having fun with
their sister.

342

Granddaughter Mikaela and fiancé Justin

Our oldest son, Nathan & his wife, Gloria's children

BENJAMIN

THOMAS

GIDEON

ELENA

Our grandson, Dagon

Our grandson, Weston

Our granddaughter, Abby

Our granddaughter, Gabby

Our grandson, Isaak

Our grandson, Isaiah

My Grandpa and Grandma Honn 1972 and 1975.
My true heroes who loved me enough to give me a home.

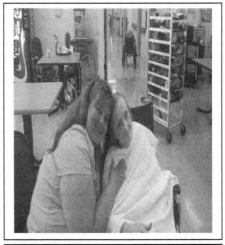

Daddy and me.
Father's Day 2017

Me & Momma; last time I
saw her. 10/22/15

Shana & her father. The 1ˢᵗ time they met. 01/04

Shana & her father, Jim and me. 06/04

Our 36ᵗʰ Wedding Anniversary July 2, 2017

POEM: BY THE SEA

By the Sea, By the Sea

My Jesus Danced with me!

By the Sea as the storms of life pulled on me, He held my hand and danced with me.

By the sea we walked on the mountains of life and in the valleys low. No matter where my life has gone my Jesus has always danced with me.

By: Tamara Gunn

ABOUT THE AUTHOR

Isaiah 52:7 Amp. How beautiful upon the mountains are the feet of him who brings good tidings who publishes peace, who brings good tidings of good, who publishes salvation, who says to Zion. Your God reigns!

Tamara M. Gunn is a minister of the Lord's. She looks forward to every opportunity given to set God's people free from bondages of fear, doubt and unbelief. She operates in the gifts of healing and prophesy. Her and her husband Bob have been married for 36 years and live in Independence Mo. They have four children and eleven grandchildren.